Faith

By
Evangelist
Robert Sanders

Son Rise Publishing
Kingsport . Tennessee
2004

Faith

*Grateful acknowledgment is given to the following for their
guidance, and help in the development of this book:*
Marlon Thomas
Jack O. Cole
Glenda Sanders
Mary Ripley

Published by: Son Rise Publishing
3717 Thorngrove Dr.
Kingsport, TN 37660
(423) 288-5773

ISBN: 978-0-9707309-3-0

Printed in the United States by Morris Publishing®
3212 East Highway 30
Kearney, NE 68847
1-800-650-7888

Table of Contents

Foreword

The Bible tell us, *" . . . without faith it is impossible to please him
. . ." (Hebrews 11:6).* We know that we are *" . . . saved by grace,
through faith . . ." (Ephesians 2:8).*

In these messages, Dr. Sanders gives us more of a comprehensive
study of faith.

As we approach the *subject* of faith, we are helped to understand
more about the *substance, structure,* and *strategy* of faith.

Dr. Sanders shows us through the scriptures, how it is possible for
our faith to be *stifled,* but also to be *strengthened.*

We see that faith brings our will in line with the *Sovereign;* and
then, the *silence* of our actions will be more effective than the
sound of our words. We learn that in the *sufficiency* of faith, our
deepest needs can be met; and we can experience the *success* of
faith in seeing God accomplish that, which is humanly impossible.

As I read these messages, I came to better appreciate the *work* of
God and the *ways* of God, which enable my *walk* with God to be
more pleasing unto Him and more effective in relation to others.

I believe that, through these messages, your apprehensions of faith
will be decreased and your appreciation of faith will be enhanced.

Through these messages, God has enabled Dr. Sanders to help us
better understand the operations of faith; thus, making it possible
for us to be more pleasing unto Him.

Dr. Marlon F. Thomas
Pastor, Sardis Baptist Church
Gainesville, Georgia

Introduction

Faith

"Therefore being justified by faith, we have peace with God through our Lord Jesus Christ" (Romans 5:1). "For therein is the righteousness of God revealed from faith to faith: as it is written, The just shall live by faith" (Romans 1:17). These two verses reveal the importance of faith. Those that are redeemed are **justified** by and they **journey** by faith. Seeing the great emphasis that God places on faith, I saw the personal need for more light. These writings are the result of my search for truth. This work is not sent forth to correct, but rather give clarity. My desire was to go beyond the theological aspect of faith that reduces faith to mere terms. I needed light on the personal and practical aspects of true Bible faith. What better way to accomplish my goal than open God's Word and look for individuals that made great statements of faith. Seeing faith in the lives of others helped me turn faith into more than some **abstract term**, but an **applicable truth**. My prayer is that God may bless these studies and that they will help you as much as they did me in my journey of faith.

Evangelist Robert Sanders D.Min.
Kingsport, Tennessee
January, 2004

Chapter One

The Subject of Faith

Hebrews 11:1-3&6 "Now faith is the substance of things hoped for, the evidence of things not seen. For by it the elders obtained a good report. Through faith we understand that the worlds were framed by the word of God, so that things which are seen were not made of things which do appear. But without faith it is impossible to please him: for he that cometh to God must believe that he is, and that he is a rewarder of them that diligently seek him."

Many do themselves a great injustice when they minimize the subject of faith. This is especially true in reference to their own personal faith. The word faith is used 247 times in 231 verses of the Bible. Of those times, 245 of them are found in the New Testament. The subject of faith is not just confined to the New Testament. *Hebrews 11* is known as the great "Hall of Faith" chapter. Within that chapter there are sixteen individuals named and set forth as examples of great faith. Of those sixteen mentioned, one half are found in one book, the book of *Genesis*, thus showing us that faith is as old as the earliest records of God's Word.

Faith must manifest itself. *James 2:17-18 "Even so faith, if it hath not works, is dead, being alone. Yea, a man may say, Thou hast faith, and I have works: show me thy faith without thy works, and I will show thee my faith by my works."* Faith is not by works, but works manifests faith! Whether named or unnamed, the heroes of faith in *Hebrews 11* reinforce the truth that living faith will make itself known. Jesus said, *"Wherefore by their fruits ye shall know them" (Matthew 7:20).* What better way to come to a greater understanding of true biblical faith than to see it manifested in the lives of others! In the furtherance of this study we will look at great statements of faith given by the life and the lips of the saints.

Before we get into the individual lives of these heroes of faith, I want us to look at faith. Let us begin our study with the subject of faith. May we gain some knowledge of faith before we make a search for it in the lives of others.

(I) The Facts About Faith – *vs.1*

Some writers have said, "in *verse 1*, we have the only place that Faith is ever defined." Others have countered by saying, "The chapter opens with words that do not constitute a definition of what faith is, but rather a statement of what faith does." To whichever view you hold, it can be safely said that *verse 1* is the greatest concentration of biblical fact concerning the subject of faith. The understanding of faith would be deficient without the truth contained within this verse! There are two facts that are projected out of this passage of scripture.

Faith is the **confident foundation of expected things**; *"Now faith is the substance of things hoped for."* The word substance has the idea of setting or placing underneath for support, hence the thought of a foundation. It also has the idea of a title deed, assurance or guarantee. Faith is not supposition, but it is substance! It is not fiction, but it is fact. Faith is not I think so, I hope so, or may be so! Vincent said, "Faith apprehends as a real fact what is not revealed to the senses. It rests on the fact, acts upon it, and is upheld by it in the face of all that seems to contradict it." Faith is an act of the mind and heart, an act of actual possession of reality. This is what a title deed implies, the actual possession of the object. Let me use this as an example of this bible truth. I am down stairs in my office. Out in front of my house is a car. I cannot physically see that car, but I know that I possess a car even if I am not setting in it and cannot see it at this time. Why? I possess the title that is free and clear to not just any car but, to that specific car in front of my house. To hold the title deed to the property is to actually possess the property!

Faith allows me to possess what God says I already possess. From God's perspective, we already possess His promises; He has already seated us in heavenly places, and we already possess eternal life *(see Ephesians 2:6)*. Faith links me to God and all His promises!

Faith is the **convicting proof of unseen things**; *"the evidence of things not seen."* The word evidence means conviction. It is a proof that conveys a satisfying conviction to the mind. It is a conviction produced by demonstration, hence we live in and by this faith *(see II Corinthians 5:7)*. It is a conviction of what we have heard but not seen with the natural eye. Faith is the opposite of sight. The world says, "seeing is believing" but faith says, "believing is seeing." This truth was projected in the life of Moses when the Bible said, *"By faith he forsook Egypt, not fearing the wrath of the king: for he endured, as **seeing him** who is invisible" (Hebrews 11:27).* We also have this record in *Hebrews 11:13, "These all died in faith, not having received the promises, but having **seen them** afar off, and were persuaded of them, and embraced them, and confessed that they were strangers and pilgrims on the earth."* Paul brings this truth out in *Romans 8:24-25, "For we are saved by hope: but hope that is seen is not hope: for what a man seeth, why doth he yet hope for? But if we hope for that we see not, then do we with patience wait for it."* Faith perceives as real fact what is not revealed to the senses. Andrew Murray said, "Just as we have our senses, through which we hold communication with the physical universe, so faith is the spiritual sense or organ through which the soul comes into contact with and is affected by the spiritual world."

Barclay said of faith, "Faith means that we are certain of the things we hope for, convinced of the things we do not see. Faith is a hope that is absolutely certain that what it believes is true, and that what it expects will come."

Wycliffe Bible Commentary says, "Faith is trust in the unseen. It is not trust in the unknown, for we may know by faith what we cannot see with the eye."

(II) The Functions of Faith – *vs.2&6a*

When thoughts turn to the function of faith, most have but one perception of faith's function and that is strictly salvation. *"For by grace are ye saved through faith" (Ephesians 2:8)*. A close detailed study of the epistles of Paul stress the importance of faith. The importance of faith for salvation must never be minimized! But, do not close the book on faith. For many, the total spectrum of faith is found within the circumference of salvation alone! We are not only given life by faith in the Lord Jesus Christ, but we live by faith, *"Now the just shall live by faith" (Hebrews 10:38)*. Faith functions in every aspect of life. Your faith is tied to earth as well as heaven and it touches every aspect of your life. While there are many more functions of faith, I want to magnify three.

The **strength of our witness** is determined by our faith. *"For by it the elders obtained a good report" (vs.2)*. The phrase *"obtained a good report"* means to be a witness, testify, give evidence, to be well reported of, to give a testimony. Our life is a testimony to the absence or the abundance of your faith. By this faith, the elders were made witnesses to the greatness and goodness of their God. They had a vibrant testimony because they had a vibrant faith. This truth can be seen in an example from the life of Peter and John. *"Now when they saw the boldness of Peter and John, and perceived that they were unlearned and ignorant men, they marvelled; and they took knowledge of them, that they had been with Jesus" (Acts 4:13)*. Peter and John were brought in before the rulers, elders, scribes, Annas the high priest, Caiaphas, John, Alexander, and many of the high priest's kindred and examined. What was the findings of the natural men? They observed two things about them. From the natural side it was obvious that Peter and John had not the benefits of higher education in the religious school of their day.

On the Godly side it was evident that they had been with Jesus for they saw Jesus in them. Christ's nature and character was projected forth from Peter and John. This powerful witness caused these rulers, elders, and scribes to marvel, to wonder and even to admire. Our witness is no greater than the quality of our faith!

Satisfying the Sovereign is determined by your faith. *"But without faith it is impossible to please him" (vs.6).* The word please means to gratify entirely or to be well pleasing to. Kenneth Wuest said, "The implication is, without faith it is impossible to please Him at all." God looks for faith in the lives of His children. The heart of our Lord was grieved on many instances as He sought faith in the lives of His disciples. A man brought his son to the disciples to be healed. Their failure projected a poor testimony that resulted in questions and a dispute. After gathering the facts about this distasteful situation Jesus said, *"O faithless and perverse generation, how long shall I be with you? how long shall I suffer you?" (Matthew 17:17).* Jesus responded to the poverty of faith in the lives of individuals by saying, *"O ye of little faith" (Matthew 8:26, 14:31, 16:8 & Luke 12:28).* In a prophetic passage on the Lord's return we are met with this question, *"Nevertheless when the Son of man cometh, shall he find faith on the earth?" (Luke 18:8).* God considers faithlessness to be sin, *"for whatsoever is not of faith is sin" (Romans 14:23).* If one desires to be well pleasing unto the Lord just manifest a strong vibrant faith. Faith is what He is looking for!

The **securing of blessings** is determined by your faith. Two blind men began to follow Jesus and to cry out for healing. They persistently followed Him down the street and into the house to hear Jesus ask them this question, *"Believe ye that I am able to do this?" (Matthew 9:28).* After answering in the affirmative, Jesus tells them that what they requested would be contingent on their faith, *"According to your faith be it unto you" (vs.29).* This principle is again seen in the life of a woman of Canaan who had a sick daughter. She was viewed by many as nothing more than a Gentile dog worthy of nothing but judgment. For days she cried after Jesus and His disciples until they being weary of her, desired that Jesus would send her away. Pleading with Jesus for even a few scraps of mercy, she heard these words, *"O woman, great is thy faith: be it unto thee even as thou wilt" (Matthew 15:28)*. Even though she was outside the commonwealth of Israel, faith prevailed. It was not in her persistence, her crying, or her wit, for they were but the personification of her faith. Faith unlocks the door to the treasure house of God's blessings. Dejected and eaten up with failure, the disciples asked Jesus why they could not heal the man's son. Jesus responded by saying, *"Because of your unbelief: for verily I say unto you, If ye have faith as a grain of mustard seed, ye shall say unto this mountain, Remove hence to yonder place; and it shall remove; and nothing shall be impossible unto you" Matthew 17:20)*. If we are to be recipients of God's bountiful blessing we must exercise faith.

Faith was needed for your salvation, but do not stop there in your faith life. You not only received life by faith, but you live life by faith! Faith functions in every aspect of your life and touches everyone around you. May each of us pray for greater faith.

(III) The Foundation of Faith – *vs. 6b*

Armed with these facts about faith and knowing the functions of faith, we must now consider the foundation of faith. Faith is founded upon truth! Void of truth, there can be no real faith. Within our text we find two foundational truths upon which biblical faith stands sure and steadfast. It is only a faith founded in these two divine truths that allows depraved humanity to approach, come near to and worship Jehovah God.

True faith is founded upon the **person of God**, *"for he that cometh to God must believe that he is."* Cometh means to approach, come near, worship, or draw near. Religion acknowledges God, but fails to draw near and worship God.

14

Many today will readily admit that there is a God, but this is not faith. Faith must lay claim to the person of God! If man is to draw near and worship God in true faith, he *"must believe that he is."* This little phrase means to have faith upon or with respect to a person, credit by implying to entrust one's spiritual well-being to Christ, to put in trust with. E.W. Bullinger said, "The common question, 'Do we believe?' is so senseless. The real question is not; 'Do we believe?' But, 'What do we believe?' or 'rather whom do we believe.'"

What is it that we are to believe about the person of God? When I read the statement, *"must believe that he is"* my heart is filled with a mixture of bewilderment and rejoicing. Bewildered by the fact that the statement is left open. God is what? While man cries for the answer to that question, no answer can be given because the nature of man cannot comprehend the fullness of who God is. Second, the majestic nature of God does not permit Him to be explained or confined to a definition. It is faith that reaches out beyond the natural senses of man and embraces the fullness of God's person. While bewildered by the absence of a definition the sense of rejoicing supersedes all other feelings because I know by faith, He will be all that I need.

By faith I embrace **His character**. There are two areas of thought that I would like to develop. Faith embraces the truth about the **uniqueness of God**. The word unique means the only one of its kind. God is not confined to a class or group for there is none to compare with Him. *"I, even I, am the LORD; and beside me there is no saviour"* (Isaiah 43:11). *"I am the LORD, and there is none else, there is no God beside me: I girded thee, though thou hast not known me: That they may know from the rising of the sun, and from the west, that there is none beside me. I am the LORD, and there is none else. For thus saith the LORD that created the heavens; God himself that formed the earth and made it; he hath established it, he created it not in vain, he formed it to be inhabited: I am the LORD; and there is none else."* (Isaiah 45:5-6 & 18). True faith does not accept that our

God is one of many, but that He is the only true and living God! Doctor Luke clears this up for us when he wrote, *"No servant can serve two masters: for either he will hate the one, and love the other; or else he will hold to the one, and despise the other. Ye cannot serve God and mammon"* (Luke 16:13). James reinforced this truth when he said, *"A double minded man is unstable in all his ways (James 1:8).*

Because our God is unique and there is none with whom He can be compared, it would be futile to try to compose a complete list of His uniqueness. A list composed of this characteristic of His nature would be endless! Therefore, I want to draw your attention to four areas that make Him unique in His nature and character. Our God is unique in His **power** for there is nothing that he can not do. God is all-powerful and He has the power to do everything that is consistent with His will and character. When speaking to His disciples, Jesus said, *"With men this is impossible; but with God all things are possible"* (Matthew 19:26). Jeremiah said, *"Ah Lord GOD! behold, thou hast made the heaven and the earth by thy great power and stretched out arm, and there is nothing too hard for thee"* (Jeremiah 32:17). Job said, *"I know that thou canst do every thing"* (Job 42:2).

The Lord is unique in His **presence**. God is everywhere present. God is everywhere active and possesses full knowledge of all that transpires in every place. William Evans said, "God is our nearest environment." While God is present in all his creation, He is in no way limited to it! David said, *"Whither shall I go from thy spirit? or whither shall I flee from thy presence? If I ascend up into heaven, thou art there: if I make my bed in hell, behold, thou art there. If I take the wings of the morning, and dwell in the uttermost parts of the sea"* (Psalm 139:7-9). While preparing His disciples for service, Jesus comforted them with these words, *"Go ye therefore . . . and, lo, I am with you alway, even unto the end of the world"* (Matthew 28:19-20).

There is the uniqueness of our God's **perception**. The Lord has infinite and perfect knowledge of all things from all eternity, whether they are actual or merely possible, whether they are past, present, or future. He has full knowledge of our thoughts. David said, *"For there is not a word in my tongue, but, lo, O LORD, thou knowest it altogether" (Psalm 139:4)*. There is not one thing that troubles our hearts or one need that arises that he is not fully aware of in each of our lives. *"For your Father knoweth what things ye have need of, before ye ask him" (Matthew 6:8)*. Joseph took comfort in knowing that God knows all things and was in charge of all things in his life. When facing his brothers and discussing their acts, Joseph said *"Now therefore be not grieved, nor angry with yourselves, that ye sold me hither: for God did send me before you to preserve life" (Genesis 45:5)*. From the hairs on our head to the future that lies ahead of each of us, God knows all things. *"For the ways of man are before the eyes of the LORD, and he pondereth all his goings" (Proverbs 5:21)*.

There is a comfort in knowing the uniqueness of His **passion**. *"Herein is love, not that we loved God, but that he loved us, and sent his Son to be the propitiation for our sins" (I John 4:10)*. The songwriter was right when he wrote, "No one ever cared for me like Jesus." *"For God so loved the world, that he gave his only begotten Son, that whosoever believeth in him should not perish, but have everlasting life. For God sent not his Son into the world to condemn the world; but that the world through him might be saved" (John 3:16-17)*. Praise be unto God for His love for sinful men and the manifestation of that love on the cross of Calvary! When we were unlovable and still rebels against God He manifested His love toward us in the person of His Son.

When it comes to His character, faith not only embraces the truth about his uniqueness, but faith embraces the truth about the **unchangeableness of God**. The believer can not only accept what God is, but they can rejoice in the fact that He will never change. *"For I am the LORD, I change not; therefore ye sons of*

Jacob are not consumed" (Malachi 3:6). James said of God's character, *"with whom is no variableness, neither shadow of turning" (James 1:17).* While you may move on the foundation of faith, the foundation will never move under you! God will not change in His **character**, in His **call** for sinners, or His **course** of future events.

By faith we embrace **His creation**. *"In the beginning was the Word, and the Word was with God, and the Word was God. The same was in the beginning with God. All things were made by him; and without him was not any thing made that was made" (John 1:1-3).* Faith not only accepts the fact that God created everything that was made, but faith sees God in all that was created. *"The heavens declare the glory of God; and the firmament showeth his handiwork" (Psalm 19:1). "The heavens declare his righteousness, and all the people see his glory" (Psalm 97:6).* True faith will not allow God to be hidden! It not only sees Him in all things, but it looks for Him in all things! The true heart of faith seeks an experiential knowledge of God. Andrew Murray wrote of this desire of faith when he said, "To know God, to see God in everything and everywhere, in our daily life, to be conscious of His presence so that we always walk with Him. Faith can walk with God."

By faith we embrace **His control**. While the natural man may question it, the person that is full of faith is well aware of the fact that God is in control. Faith **acknowledges** God's control. Many look at this vast cosmos filled with its inhabitants and attribute it all to cause and effect. It is like a line of dominos, one falling on the other void of reasoning or restraint. Among their favorite words is the word chance! These individuals see no hand at the wheel, no governing force with a definite plan in anything. While it is understandable for the natural man groping in the darkness of depravity to hold this distorted view, it is inexcusable for the children of light. Faith looks beyond this world and sees God reigning upon His throne and ruling in the affairs of all men. We read of His control in the book of Isaiah,

"The LORD of hosts hath sworn, saying, Surely as I have thought, so shall it come to pass; and as I have purposed, so shall it stand: . . . For the LORD of hosts hath purposed, and who shall disannul it? and his hand is stretched out, and who shall turn it back?" (Isaiah 14:24&27). Paul reminds us that God *"worketh all things after the counsel of his own will" (see Ephesians 1:11).* There is more than just a hand on the wheel; there is a capable hand on the wheel. Nothing lies outside the boundary of His control!

It is the delight of faith to **accept** God's control. Filled with faith rather than fear, the believer can say with the Apostle Paul, *"And we know that all things work together for good to them that love God, to them who are the called according to his purpose" (Romans 8:28).* Faith trusts God to do all things well! While the decrees of God may be beyond the ability of man to perceive them, faith rests in them because they are **eternal** and **immutable**. *"The counsel of the LORD standeth for ever, the thoughts of his heart to all generations" (Psalm 33:11).* God made the decrees in eternity past, and nothing has happened or can happen to change them! God is not seated in heaven scrutinizing the activities of the world trying to figure out what He is going to do next. He has and forever will be in control. Faith rests in the decrees of God because they are **holy** and **wise**. *"The LORD is righteous in all his ways, and holy in all his works" (Pslam 145:17).* Faith can rest in the decrees of God because it will bring Him **glory** and be for our **good** *(see Romans 8:28).* True biblical faith goes beyond acknowledging God's control, but it rests in the acceptance of God's control.

We now come to the second foundational truth of Bible faith. True faith is founded upon the **promises of God**, *"that he is a rewarder of them that diligently seek him."* Faith in the person of God must precede faith in the promises of God. Your ability to embrace the promise is only as good as your confidence of the person making the promise. This God of character, creation and control *"is a rewarder of them that diligently seek him."*

19

Diligently seek means to search out, investigate, crave, demand, to worship, to seek after carefully and diligently. This is not a passive act, one that lacks energy or desire, rather it is one of passionate desire and hunger. It is exhibited in the life of David when he said, *"As the hart panteth after the water brooks, so panteth my soul after thee, O God. My soul thirsteth for God, for the living God: when shall I come and appear before God?" (Psalm 42:1-2)*. Faith does not look to God as a last **resort**; it looks to God as the only **resource**! *"Every good gift and every perfect gift is from above, and cometh down from the Father of lights, with whom is no variableness, neither shadow of turning" (James 1:17)*.

God is described as a *"rewarder."* The word comes from two words, the first meaning giver of gifts, to pay a person for work done, to give away, to deliver, recompense, or give again. The second word means to let out for wages or hire. The thought before us is that all, who turn to God, will not be disappointed. Those that come will receive! *"Come unto me, all ye that labour and are heavy laden, and I will give you rest" (Matthew 11:28)*. Those that call will get an answer. *"Call unto me, and I will answer thee, and show thee great and mighty things, which thou knowest not" (Jeremiah 33:3)*. God will never fail!

Andrew Murray said, "Faith believes that God can be found; that He can and will make Himself known . . . that He has a divine reward for the seeker after Him. In seeking Him the way may at times be dark and long, and the progress slow: faith honors God with its confidence as the God of love and truth; He will reward and bless. Let the deep restfulness of this assured conviction be the root of all your seeking after God." Faith in God's person and God's promises are the foundation of biblical faith. William Newell said, "These elements seem most simple, but, alas, how many professing Christians act as if God were not living; and how many others, though seeking after Him, are not expecting from Him as Rewarder!"

Are you a person of faith? To neglect one's faith is to neglect one's Christian life. Faith not only wrought salvation but it sustains, supplies, and sanctifies the believer's life. To minimize and neglect faith is a sin *"for whatsoever is not of faith is sin"* *(Romans 14:23).*

Chapter Two

The Substance of Faith

Matthew 8:7-8 "And Jesus saith unto him, I will come and heal him. The centurion answered and said, Lord, I am not worthy that thou shouldest come under my roof: but speak the word only, and my servant shall be healed."
Romans 10:17 "So then faith cometh by hearing, and hearing by the word of God."

When the writer of *Hebrews* used the word *"substance"* in *Hebrews 11:1*, it was in reference to the confident foundation of things that were expected. Here I want to use a different thought when I use the word "substance." Webster defines the word as the real or essential part of anything, the essence, the physical matter of which a thing consists, matter of a particular kind. Let me use an example to explain what I mean. The substance of water consists of two elements, hydrogen and oxygen. Every molecule of water consists of two atoms of hydrogen and one atom of oxygen. By removing one of these elements or adding an element to them, it would no longer be water! If the hydrogen is removed it leaves pure oxygen, which is very flammable. One would then have oxygen to breathe, but no water to drink. If sulfur and more oxygen were added to the water it would create sulfuric acid, which is very caustic and deadly. This is an example of what has created such havoc and tragedy in the realm of religion. Some are discarding certain essential elements of faith, while others are adding to the mixture. In both cases lives are being lost and destroyed by the creation of an unbiblical faith!

Because of this degenerative faith, many are dying of spiritual thirst. In *John 6:35*, Jesus spoke of a faith that could satisfy all thirst, *"he that believeth on me shall never thirst."* Others dispense a caustic brew distilled by human wisdom and bottled in fleshly works. This hideous brew burns and destroys all that come in contact with it. In *Luke 18:11*, Jesus tells of a caustic faith, *"The Pharisee stood and prayed thus with himself, God, I thank thee, that I am not as other men are, extortioners, unjust, adulterers, or even as this publican."* Whether it is the absence of water or the dispensing of poison the outcome remains the same. Ultimately they die!

We have recorded for us in *Matthew 8 & Luke 7*, the account of Christ healing the centurion's servant. In this account a great statement of faith is found concerning the substance of faith, *"but speak the word only, and my servant shall be healed" (Matthew 8:7)*. The centurion was acting out in his life what the Apostle Paul would one day say with his lips, *"So then faith cometh by hearing, and hearing by the word of God" (Romans 10:17)*. Through the centurion's life, we see in practice, the principle of what Paul would one day deliver concerning the substance of faith. There are two principle elements to true biblical faith. Neither of these elements can be discarded and nothing can be added if it is to be real faith.

(I) The Acquisition of Truth – *"cometh by hearing"*

Biblical faith is forever a sure faith because it is founded upon truth. In order to exhibit true faith, there must be the acquisition of truth! What is God's method of acquiring this truth? Roy Laurin said, "We do not get faith by asking, but by hearing. We do not get it by reasoning, but by revelation." William Newell said, "If you hear, with a willing heart . . . by truly *'hearing'*, faith will 'come' to you. You do not have to do a thing but hear!" The tragedy among men is that they refuse to hear. Again and again from the lips of the Lord Jesus Christ we hear the admonition to be a hearer, *"He that hath ears to hear, let him hear"(Matthew 11:15, 13:9&43)*. With this thought in mind, there are two things that call for our attention. There is the **necessity of hearing.** In *Luke's* account of the healing of the centurion's servant, you find these words, *"And when he heard* *of Jesus, he sent unto him the elders of the Jews, beseeching him that he would come and heal his servant" (Luke 7:3).* Like all those that preceded him, and all those that would follow, if faith were to flourish in the life of this man he must hear with his heart and not his intellect. From the biblical accounts we conclude that the centurion heard of the Lord's **person.** This may be seen in the means he used to approach Christ, *"he sent unto him the elders of the Jews, beseeching him that he would come and heal his servant" (Luke 7:3).* What he had heard about the Lord caused him to esteem the Lord above other men, which was manifested in acts of humility. He was humble in **making his request,** *"Wherefore neither thought I myself worthy to come unto thee" (Luke 7:7).* He felt unworthy to even come before the Lord and ask Him to heal his servant. His humility was seen in the **entering of his residence,** *"I am not worthy that thou shouldest enter under my roof" (Luke 7:6).* While the elders of the Jews were saying this centurion is worthy and listing all his great accomplishments *(see Luke 7:4-5),* the centurion was crying unworthy, unworthy, unworthy!

The centurion had heard of the Lord's **power.** The centurion knew in his heart that he was not requesting anything outside the dominion of our Lord's power. Because he had heard something of Jesus' person, the centurion knew that such a person occupied a lofty position and with that position came the power. This centurion knew the power of the spoken word *(see Matthew 8:8-9).*

While it was necessary to hear of the Lord's person and His power, the thing that delighted the heart of this man was the Lord's **presence.** Jesus was near! Jesus had come to where this man was, *"he entered into Capernaum" (Luke 7:1).* Thank God for the glorious truth that "God has always moved toward man!" Are not these words of Jesus an encouragement to the hearts of Adam's race, *"I am come that they might have life, and that they might have it more abundantly" (John 10:10).* What good would it be to know a person of prestige and power if they were totally inaccessible? Christ, the man of power and prominence had drawn near and the centurion was going to respond. When man had no way to approach God, God moved in the direction of those undeserving creatures. The centurion heard of Jesus!

There is the **necessity of being heard.** Someone had to speak to the centurion about the Lord Jesus Christ. It is the responsibility of all men to hear, but it is our responsibility to tell all men! W.M. Hubbard said, "While many hear but do not believe, those who believe have first heard." While we are not provided with the name or names of those that were faithful to witness of our Lord's great power, we do know that someone did. *"Let the redeemed of the LORD say so, whom he hath redeemed from the hand of the enemy" (Psalm 107:2).*

Knowing the importance of hearing, the Apostle Paul wrote these words, *"How then shall they call on him in whom they have not believed? and how shall they believe in him of whom they have not heard? and how shall they hear without a preacher?" (Romans 10:14).* The word preacher means to herald as a public crier the divine truth of the gospel. It is the responsibility of all those that have been redeemed by God's marvelous grace to spread the good news. When writing to the church at Corinth, Paul told them, all that have been reconciled unto God have been given the ministry and the word of reconciliation *(see II Corinthians 5:18-20).* We have no right to expect God to save our loved one's if we are not willing to take the responsibility of telling them!

In pursuing the truth, have we been faithful to **hear** and have we been faithful to **herald** the truth?

(II) The Allocation of Truth – *"hearing by the word of God"*
While there is a premium on hearing, one must not forget the second element is equally important! What one hears is as important as the fact that one does hear. When I think of this

aspect of faith, the woman with the issue of blood comes to mind. Listen to this statement from the Word of God, *"And had suffered many things of many physicians, and had spent all that she had, and was nothing bettered, but rather grew worse" (Mark 5:26).* Why do you think she had gone to all those different doctors? Someone told her that they could give her relief from the disease that had plagued her life for twelve years! She had been faithful to hear, but the problem was in what she heard. Please get the ramifications of this statement; *"was nothing bettered."* In fact she was worse off because the treatments had not only inflicted greater suffering, but also depleted all her resources! Many individuals are suffering and spiritually bankrupt not because they have failed to hear, but they have not been given the truth!

I want to ask a question and please think carefully before you answer. Was there any other solution to the centurion's problem other than the intervention of God? If you believe there was, you have a big problem. The centurion not only had to hear with an open heart, but he had to hear the truth. Where does one find truth? The allocation of truth is the Word of God! Paul said, *"faith cometh by hearing, and hearing by the word of God."* Roy Laurin said, "The origin of faith is in the Word of God. Just as the red corpuscles of the blood stream are manufactured in the marrow of our bones, so faith is produced in the heart of the Bible. Out of these divine truths rises our strength." It was a word from God that would alter the centurion's situation and God's Word alone.

The centurion not only knew the importance of the spoken word, but the importance of who was speaking. *"For I am a man under authority, having soldiers under me: and I say to this man, Go, and he goeth; and to another, Come, and he cometh; and to my servant, Do this, and he doeth it" (Matthew 8:9).* When I tell a soldier to go, he goes. When I tell a soldier to come, he comes. That soldier responds to the spoken word because of the authority behind that word. Because that soldier is under me, I have the authority to issue commands and he obeys because of my authority. The centurion knew that Jesus did not have to be present to heal his servant. The spoken word of Jesus would be sufficient because it was an **authoritative word**. Spurgeon said, "The centurion's unstaggering faith required no crutch. He believed that diseases had to obey Christ's bidding just as he had to obey his superior officers."

In the account of creation we have seven specific times that God spoke. These specific times are marked by the phrase, *"God said" (see Genesis 1:3, 6, 9, 11, 14, 20 & 24).* Every time God spoke things happened just like He spoke it. While on this earth Jesus spoke to the boisterous sea and it lay down quietly at His feet. Listen to the testimony of our Lord's disciples, *"What manner of man is this! for he commandeth even the winds and water, and they obey him" (Luke 8:25).* Jesus spoke to the lifeless body of a young maid and she arose. He spoke to a deceptive fig tree and it withered away. He spoke to the angry mob in the garden and they fell backwards. If Jesus would but speak to the diseased body of his servant, the centurion knew it would be made whole. It would happen because Jesus' word was one of authority.

The centurion not only knew something of the **span** of authority, but something of the **season** of authority. Not only was everything under the centurion subject to obeying him, but also as long as he occupied that position he would possess the authority, which demanded obedience. The centurion knew that all things were under the authority of Jesus' words no matter when He spoke them. Jesus said concerning the season of God's Word, *"For verily I say unto you, Till heaven and earth pass, one jot or one tittle shall in no wise pass from the law, till all be fulfilled" (Matthew 5:18).* The Psalmist said, *"For ever, O LORD, thy word is settled in heaven" (Psalm 119:89).* If God said it, that settles it!

If the centurion's servant were to be healed, it would require true biblical faith. The faith needed would consist of two elements, hearing with a willing heart and hearing the truth of God's Word. To delete either element or add to the compound would mean death, suffering, and depletion of resources. Do you possess the substance that true faith is made of?

Chapter Three

The Structure of Faith

Luke 7:50 "And he said to the woman, Thy faith hath saved thee; go in peace."

Doctor Luke places before us an account of great faith! The setting is in the house of a Pharisee. Jesus has been invited to come and partake of a meal with the Pharisee and his friends. Accepting the invitation, Jesus enters *"and sat down to meat" (Luke 7:36)*. Onlookers have gathered in the street to watch the festivities. Then suddenly a woman came out of the crowd bearing an alabaster box and stood behind Jesus. Falling at His feet, she *"began to wash his feet with tears, and did wipe them with the hairs of her head, and kissed his feet, and anointed them with the ointment" (Luke 7:38)*. Every eye was now upon her and the one with whom she so affectionately administered her devotion. While unnamed in the text, she was not unknown to those about the table. There are at least three details we can gather about this woman at Jesus feet. She was a **resident** of the city. She had a **reputation** of being a very sinful individual. And she exhibited a **repentant** spirit before the Lord. The thing that preoccupied the minds of her critics was her reputation, *"which was a sinner" (vs. 37)*, and not her repentance.

The self-righteous could not get past her **failures**, while Jesus could not dismiss her **faith**. We have no record of her saying anything with her lips; yet she makes a great statement of faith with her life. Jesus said, *"Thy faith hath saved thee."* True faith had carried her from the **mire of sin**, to the **mercies of salvation**. The Pharisees were interested in exposing transgressions while Jesus was there to eradicate transgressions; *"And their sins and iniquities will I remember no more" (Hebrews 10:17)*. The ceremonial-clean focused on outward transgressions and dismissed the wickedness of their inward thoughts. Jesus said of this mentality, *"Woe unto you, scribes and Pharisees, hypocrites! for ye are like unto whited sepulchres, which indeed appear beautiful outward, but are within full of dead men's bones, and of all uncleanness"* (Matthew 23:27).

Those who had gathered for the meal had failed to understand that all were sinners. *"For all have sinned, and come short of the glory of God" (Romans 3:23). "There is none righteous, no, not one: There is none that understandeth, there is none that seeketh after God. They are all gone out of the way, they are together become unprofitable; there is none that doeth good, no, not one"* (Romans 3:10-12). There was only one difference between the prosperous Pharisee and the polluted prostitute, one was a righteous sinner and the other was a repulsive sinner. Both were under the condemnation of a Holy God! All had the same affliction requiring the same cure, why did only one leave justified and the others remained under divine judgment? Jesus tells us the answer, *"Thy faith hath saved thee; go in peace"* (Luke 7:50). Faith sent her home forgiven, *"Thy sins are forgiven"* (Luke 7:48).

What was it that constituted faith in this sinful prostitute and not in the sanctimonious Pharisee? There are three elements that are involved in the structure of faith. Each one of these elements can be seen within our text. Those elements do not die with the story, but are exhibited in the lives of all that exercise faith. A.W. Pink said, "The man within the body is possessed of three principal faculties: the understanding, the affections, and the will." All three of these must come together in a corporate manner for faith to flourish in the life of an individual. I want us to examine the three elements that makeup the **structure of faith**: the intellect, the affections, and the will.

(I) Their Corruption

When one begins to study the intellect, the affections, and the will, it is necessary to remember that these three elements are found in the unregenerate as well as in those of faith. The same three elements that lead some to **pardon** will lead others to **perdition**. All of us possess intellect, affections, and a will. If this were the case, then why doesn't every one accept the Lord Jesus Christ as their Saviour? Our intellect, affections, and will have been corrupted by the fall. Sin has tainted those three elements as well as many other areas in each of our lives.

Man in his natural state after the fall has a corrupt intellect or mind. When writing to the believers at Ephesus, he admonished them to live a life that was indicative of the spiritual man and not that of the natural man. *"This I say therefore, and testify in the Lord, that ye henceforth walk not as other Gentiles walk, in the vanity of their mind, Having the understanding darkened, being alienated from the life of God through the ignorance that is in them, because of the blindness of their heart" (Ephesians 4:17-18).* In this text Paul makes three graphic statements about man in his fallen state and each of them have to do with the intellect. Paul said that the *"other Gentiles walk, in the vanity of their mind."* The word *"mind"* means the intellect, the mind or understanding. This intellect is in a state of *"vanity"* which means depravity or corrupt morally. Thus, man has a morally corrupt intellect. Paul describes them as *"Having the understanding darkened." "Understanding"* has reference to the faculty of the mind and its disposition. Paul said that disposition of the mind was *"darkened"* which means to obscure, to make vague or not well known. Spiritual things are foreign to the intellect of the natural man. The last descriptive phrase is *"blindness of their heart."* The word *"heart"* means the thoughts and feelings of the mind. Paul describes the heart, as being in a state of *"blindness"* which is one of stupidity or callousness. If one were to combine the terms that Paul used to describe the intellect of the natural man it would be a person whose intellect has been corrupted morally and is hardened and ignorant to the spiritual things of God. While the Pharisee in our story may not want to admit it, this is an accurate description of his intellect as well as our own.

The fallen man has corrupt affections. Our corrupt affections are the results of a corrupt intellect. *"There is none that understandeth, there is none that seeketh after God" (Romans 3:11).* The little phrase *"seeketh after,"* means to search out, to have a craving for, to demand, to seek after carefully or diligently. John put it this way, *"And this is the condemnation, that light is come into the world, and men loved darkness rather than light" (John 3:19).* The object of man's affections is self rather than the Saviour! John the beloved wrote, *"Love not the world, neither the things that are in the world. If any man love the world, the love of the Father is not in him. For all that is in the world, the lust of the flesh, and the lust of the eyes, and the pride of life, is not of the Father, but is of the world" (I John 2:15-16).* Why would we have such an admonishment if the natural affections of man were not corrupted with a desire for the things of the world rather than the things of God? Man's love for God is reciprocal, *"We love him, because he first loved us" (I John 4:19).* Our affections for Him are in response to His great love for us.

The natural man has a corrupt will. When speaking to the Jews that desired to kill Him, Jesus said, *"And ye will not come to me, that ye might have life" (John 5:40).* The word John uses for *"will"* has the idea of a determined act as opposed to an impulse. Man's will is set against God and the things of God. Jesus said, *"No man can come to me, except the Father which hath sent me draw him" (John 6:44).* No man has the ability or the power to come to Christ because they have no desire for or see the need for Christ. Our will is turned against Him because our affections are set on pleasing self and we are totally absorbed with self because of an intellect that is morally corrupt and hardened against God.

The Pharisee may have been religious and inquisitive but he was lost. As he scrutinized the actions of this sinful woman it was one of **contrast** and not **comparison**. He perceived himself as being totally different and God saw them as being similar. *"They are all gone out of the way, they are together become unprofitable; there is none that doeth good, no, not one" (Romans 3:12).* Paul used the phrase, *"there is none"* three times in *Romans 3; "There is none righteous" (vs. 10), "There is none that understandeth" (vs. 11), "there is none that seeketh after God" (vs. 12).* It is not a pleasant thought, but each of us is not in contrast to the sinful prostitute or the sanctimonious Pharisee, but we are in companionship with them. We are sinners by nature! Thus, corrupt in our intellect, our affections, and our will.

(II) Their Cleansing

If this woman is totally corrupt in her intellect, her affections, and her will because of the fall, how was it possible that she could exhibit saving faith? There can only be one and only one possible answer to that question! Something had to cleanse the corrupt nature of these elements. What could possibly do such a tremendous feat? The answer is not in a what, but a who! The Holy Spirit has been dispatched to this sinful world to call out a bride for the Son. *"And when he is come, he will reprove the world of sin, and of righteousness, and of judgment" (John 16:8).* When the Holy Spirit came He set about admonishing, convicting, and convincing man. How we praise the Lord for a God that loves sinners. Our God has always actively sought out wayward man. It was God seeking out Adam in the garden, *"And the LORD God called unto Adam, and said unto him, Where art thou?" (Genesis 3:9).* God called out Abraham from among his idols, *"Now the LORD had said unto Abram, Get thee out of thy country, and from thy kindred, and from thy father's house, unto a land that I will show thee: And I will make of thee a great nation, and I will bless thee, and make thy name great; and thou shalt be a blessing" (Genesis 12:1-2).* Jesus said, *"For the Son of man is come to seek and to save that which was lost"*

(Luke 19:10). When man was unwilling and incapable of moving toward God, that God motivated by love and mercy moved toward man!

The Holy Spirit begins His work on this woman's intellect. *"And, behold, a woman in the city, which was a sinner, when she knew that Jesus sat at meat in the Pharisee's house" (Luke 7:37).* Please note the little phrase, *"when she knew." "Knew"* means to know as the result of some mark, to recognize by implying to become fully acquainted with, to acknowledge. While Simon may have not been fully aware of who had come for a visit, there was one that did and she would not let the opportunity escape her. The Holy Spirit came to make known the Lord Jesus Christ. *"But when the Comforter is come . . . he shall testify of me" (John 15:26). "Howbeit when he, the Spirit of truth . . . he shall not speak of himself . . . He shall glorify me: for he shall receive of mine, and shall show it unto you" (John 16:13-14).* This great truth can be clearly seen in the life on Simeon in *Luke 2.* Mary and Joseph had taken Jesus to Jerusalem to offer a sacrifice in accordance to the law of the Lord *(see Luke 2:21-24).* While they were in the Temple Simeon came into the Temple and saw the child Jesus. What was his response to seeing this small infant? *"Then took he him up in his arms, and blessed God . . . mine eyes have seen thy salvation" (Luke 2:28-30).* How did he know that this was the Son of God, the one that should come into the world to redeem fallen humanity? There are three descriptive phrases that tell us a great deal about Simeon and this event: *"the Holy Ghost was upon him", "And it was revealed unto him by the Holy Ghost",* and *"And he came by the Spirit" (vs. 25-27).* The Spirit of God gave enlightenment to Simeon so he would know Jesus when he saw Him. Satan is in the business of blinding the minds of the people, and the Spirit is in the business of giving light. *"In whom the god of this world hath blinded the minds of them which believe not, lest the light of the glorious gospel of Christ, who is the image of God, should shine unto them" (II Corinthians 4:4).* The same Holy Spirit that revealed Jesus unto

Simeon has revealed Jesus to this wicked woman and He is still making Jesus known to the fallen of Adam's race.

After the intellect has been given light as to the person of Christ, the affections begin to draw one's heart to Christ. Why is this woman willing to subject herself to the criticism of these religious Pharisees? What would cause her to leave the shadows of concealment to have her sins exposed in the light? The answer may be too simplistic for some, but the truth is she wants to be near Jesus. Her affections have been turned away from self and unto the Saviour. Entering the house she stands silently behind Him. A hush has come over everyone and the only sound to be heard is the compassionate sobs of her broken heart. Tears stream down her face as she looks upon Him. In tenderness she bows and begins to kiss His feet and rub them with the hair of her head.

Her affections must now manifest themselves by an act of the will. A love for self would have kept her groping in the darkness seeking to satisfy the appetites of the flesh. Her affections had been changed by her knowledge of Him. Everything she was now doing was motivated by affections for Him. Jesus points out that the difference between the actions of Simon and those of this penitent prostitute was love! Jesus said of Simon, *"thou gavest me no water"* and *"thou gavest me no kiss" (vs. 44&45).* While Simon was withholding from Jesus the objects of common courtesy, the object of Simon's scorn was lavishing upon Jesus all that she possessed mentally, emotionally and monetarily. *"Seest thou this woman . . . she hath washed my feet with tears, and wiped them with the hairs of her head . . . this woman since the time I came in hath not ceased to kiss my feet" (Luke 7:44-47).*

The songwriter, Squire Parsons, was theologically sound when he wrote, "When I could not go to where He was He came to me." Bound in the quagmire of sin, the sinner cannot help himself. But, thanks be unto God for His great love that would

35

cause Him to move toward such lowly creatures as you and I. *"But God commendeth his love toward us, in that, while we were yet sinners, Christ died for us" (Romans 5:8)*. While we were yet sinners, God was working in our behalf. God is pleased to do for us what we cannot do for ourselves.

(III) Their Cooperation

As we examine this great example of faith in this woman's life we have looked closely at the structure of faith. We have looked at the intellect, the affections, and the will. While we have dealt with them as individual elements in the structure of faith, they do not work independently of each other. It is only in their corporate action that faith is manifested. There are some that would major on one element and call it faith. The hirelings of the world have not only sowed this subtle lie into many hearts, but much of the seed has come up and is corrupting the church of today.

There are those that perceive faith as nothing more than an intellectual decision. Man simply gathers all the facts and by the means of logic one determines the proper course of action. When writing to the church at Corinth, Paul said, *"And my speech and my preaching was not with enticing words of man's wisdom, but in demonstration of the Spirit and of power: That your faith should not stand in the wisdom of men, but in the power of God" (1 Corinthians 2:4-5)*. Paul wanted those at Corinth to know that he had not come to them with persuasive words and methods after the manner of men's wisdom. Paul was not using the world's methods with a simple religious twist to it. This is much of what we see today. The religious fervor of today is the importance of **methods** over the **message**. Studies are done on successful business practices; the principles outlined with a few Bible verses sprinkled in for taste and you have an instant church growth seminar that guarantees success. Those that are fond of these methods usually draw men to themselves rather than draw men to God. When Paul uses the word *"stand"* it means to exist or to have been. Paul points out that there are only two kinds of faith, one that exists in man and one that exists in God. Paul was well equipped to address this aspect of faith. His entire religious experience was once built around the intellectual wisdom of men. Listen as he describes this intellectual state he once enjoyed. *"I am verily a man which am a Jew, born in Tarsus, a city in Cilicia, yet brought up in this city at the feet of Gamaliel, and taught according to the perfect manner of the law of the fathers, and was zealous toward God, as ye all are this day" (Acts 22:3).* Paul had the advantage of studying under the best that man had to offer and at best it was still just man! Listen to what was said about some uneducated fishermen. *Now when they saw the boldness of Peter and John, and perceived that they were unlearned and ignorant men, they marvelled; and they took knowledge of them, that they had been with Jesus" (Acts 4:13).* If faith is to flourish in one's life it must begin with **spiritual enlightenment** and not in **superior education**.

While some would make faith totally an intellectual experience, others would cast aside enlightenment for emotionalism! For them faith is totally in one's affections. There is a strong movement today to discount the **quality of the message** for a **quantity of merriment**. They meet regularly for a foot stomping, hand clapping religious hoedown. They do not come to hear something but rather to feel something! The test of the preaching and the service is not did I hear the Word of God, but rather how did it make me feel. Did I get my religious-hi for the week? One cannot always trust human affections! The same crowd that cried *"Hosanna to the son of David: Blessed is he that cometh in the name of the Lord; Hosanna in the highest" (Matthew 21:19)* would soon cry, *"His blood be on us, and on our children" (Matthew 27:25).* The Bible still says, *"The heart is deceitful above all things, and desperately wicked: who can know it?" (Jeremiah 17:9).* Faith goes beyond the **human senses** and trusts the **Holy Scriptures**. Faith is not without feelings, but it is not based on feelings!

Throwing out the intellect and the affections, some see faith as purely an act of the human will. One simply wills to be saved or I just decide one day that I will get saved. When speaking of the recipients of great salvation, John said, *"But as many as received him, to them gave he power to become the sons of God, even to them that believe on his name: Which were born, not of blood, nor of the will of the flesh, nor of the will of man, but of God" (John 1:12-13)*. John tells us that faith is not simply the determination, inclination, desire or pleasure of man's will.

It is only when the intellect, the affections, and the will, under the divine influence of the Holy Spirit, work in a corporate manner is faith manifested. Each one of these has to be actively involved if one is to exercise true biblical faith.

(IV) Their Continuance

When this woman leaves Simon's house it is with full knowledge that her sins have been forgiven and she has new life in Christ, *"Thy faith hath saved thee; go in peace" (Luke 7:50)*. Faith has flourished into everlasting life. She has begun the journey with faith and if that life is to be enriched, it must continue in faith. *"The just shall live by faith" (Romans 1:17)*. A man of faith today may not be a man of faith tomorrow. I say this not in respect to our salvation, but rather the stewardship of the life God has given His children. The Father of faith, Abraham, is a good example of this truth. We see an act of faith when he turns his back on his homeland with its ways and its people to follow the True and Living God. It was faith that would cause him to have *"sojourned in the land of promise, as in a strange country, dwelling in tabernacles with Isaac and Jacob, the heirs with him of the same promise: For he looked for a city which hath foundations, whose builder and maker is God" (Hebrews 11:9-10)*. But, faith did not take him down into Egypt in the time of famine. Faith did not cause him to lie about Sarah being his wife. It was not faith that sent him unto the bed of Hagar.

If there is to be a steady walk of faith in the life of this woman, there must be a continuance in the corporate action of the intellect, affections, and the will. What is true for her is true for all of God's children. Failure in the faith-life is due to a breakdown in either our intellect, our affections, or our will. Our faith cannot flourish and mature from little faith to great faith if we cease to expand our knowledge of Him. Just as we could not have faith in a God we did not know, our faith cannot advance without a greater knowledge of His person, His power, His purpose, and His promises. The foundation of faith is the Word of God, *"So then faith cometh by hearing, and hearing by the word of God" (Romans 10:17).* Thus, if the structure of faith is to be enlarged, so must the foundation! For many the journey of faith has been stifled because of a neglect of the preaching, teaching and study of God's Word. New faith cannot be instituted because it has nothing to stand upon! That moment any child of God stops taking in the Word, their faith-life begins to deteriorate.

If faith is to continually gain ground the affection must remain true to God. *"Love not the world, neither the things that are in the world. If any man love the world, the love of the Father is not in him. For all that is in the world, the lust of the flesh, and the lust of the eyes, and the pride of life, is not of the Father, but is of the world" (I John 2:15-16).* It is so easy for the affections to be corrupted by a love of self. The songwriter, Robert Robinson, was right when he penned the words to the song "Come, Thou Fount." He said, "Prone to wander, Lord I feel it, prone to leave the God I love." The heart of man is so fickle! When speaking to the church of Ephesus, God commended them for their works, their labors, and their patience. But, closed with this admonition, *"Nevertheless I have somewhat against thee, because thou hast left thy first love" (Revelations 2:4).* While busy with their hands, they were indifferent with their hearts. It did not say that they had ceased to love God. He had just ceased to occupy first place in their lives. The disciples had become preoccupied with substance at the expense of spiritual matters.

Jesus tells them to change their priorities and *"seek ye first the kingdom of God" (Matthew 6:33)*. Self, substance, Satan, and sin can corrupt the affections of our hearts. These are a deterrent to the manifestation as well as the maturing of our faith.

Faith can only flourish when our will is in obedience to His will. If one finds themselves in opposition to the will of God, the ways of God and the Word of God, one can safely surmise that they are not walking in faith. True faith responds positively to the known will of God. *"Therefore to him that knoweth to do good, and doeth it not, to him it is sin" (James 4:17)*. Failing to act on the Word indicates an absence of faith.

We not only obtain spiritual life by faith; we nourish that life by faith. Whether it is a sinner in the gaining of life, or a saint in the enrichment of that life, faith must be active. To do so requires the continual cooperation of the intellect, the affections and the will. Together they manifest faith in our lives. To neglect any one of these elements means the absence of faith. May we cry with the Apostle Paul, *"That I may know him, and the power of his resurrection, and the fellowship of his sufferings" (Philippians 3:10)*. May the affections of our heart be that of the first and greatest of God's commandments, *"Thou shalt love the Lord thy God with all thy heart, and with all thy soul, and with all thy mind" (Matthew 22:37)*. And may we adhere to the admonishment of Mary to the servants, *"Whatsoever he saith unto you, do it" (John 2:5)*. While the intellect, the affections, and the will are not faith in and of themselves, they must through a corporate action be affected if faith is to be manifested.

Chapter Four

The Strategy of Faith

Luke 5:4-5 "Now when he had left speaking, he said unto Simon, Launch out into the deep, and let down your nets for a draught. And Simon answering said unto him, Master, we have toiled all the night, and have taken nothing: nevertheless at thy word I will let down the net."

One dictionary defines strategy as a carefully worked out plan of action. If this is the case, what is faith's plan of action? The answer to this very important question can be seen in this statement made by Simon Peter. *"Master, we have toiled all the night, and have taken nothing: nevertheless at thy word I will let down the net."* True biblical faith has but one and only one plan of action, obedience to God's Word!

True biblical faith desires to know but one thing, "what wilt thou have me to do?" This is the response of the infamous Saul of Tarsus at his conversion, *"And he trembling and astonished said, Lord, what wilt thou have me to do? And the Lord said unto him, Arise, and go into the city, and it shall be told thee what thou must do" (Acts 9:6).* Once the Word has been delivered to the heart of the individual, faith will do but one thing, obey! Listen to Simon Peter's great statement of faith; *"at thy word I will."* In spite of the conflict between **self-will** and the **Sovereign's will** faith rises to the occasion and submits to the authority of the Word. Faith thrives on pleasing God and doing His will.

Faith is not so much in saying but in doing. Listen to the words of our Lord, *"But what think ye? A certain man had two sons; and he came to the first, and said, Son, go work to day in my vineyard. He answered and said, I will not: but afterward he repented, and went. And he came to the second, and said likewise. And he answered and said, I go, sir: and went not. Whether of them twain did the will of his father? They say unto him, The first" Matthew 21:28-31).* Oration is no substitute for obedience!

While it is the strategy of true faith to obey, that willingness to obey will not go unchallenged. Though it may be challenged, it will not be conquered. We find this to be true in the life of Simon Peter. Faith says, *"I will"* to *"Thy will."*

(I) The Vision of Obedience – vs.5 *Master*

Who is this one that has just issued an order to *"Launch out into the deep, and let down your nets for a draught" (Luke 5:4)*? Is he a Rabbi or just another one of those religious radicals that has come on the scene for a short season? Peter makes reference to Jesus as *"Master."* In the New Testament, the word master is used 72 times in 68 verses. In most references where the word is used, the writer uses a standard generic term for the word master. It has the idea of an instructor and comes from a word that means to cause to learn or to teach. This was a word that was used by almost anyone with reference to almost everyone. While it may have been a respectful word, it carried very little weight.

Simon does not use the standard generic term, but choose a different word. It appears that Simon is the first to use this word in respect to the Lord Jesus Christ. He uses the word "epistates," which means an appointee over or commander. Simon Peter has come to realize that this one with whom he occupies the ship is no ordinary individual. Simon is not standing in the presence of one that is his equal but rather his superior! Simon has made a startling discovery. Jesus is not only giving commands, but as the appointee over and the commander of all things, He has every right to do so.

Most of us would see our faith flourish if we were to have a fresh vision of Christ. No man can stay the same after a personal encounter with the God of heaven. When Isaiah saw the Lord he **spoke with remorse,** *"Woe is me! for I am undone; because I am a man of unclean lips, and I dwell in the midst of a people of unclean lips: for mine eyes have seen the King, the LORD of hosts" (Isaiah 6:5).* When John the beloved saw the Lord he was **smitten with reverence,** *"I fell at his feet as dead" (Revelation 1:17).* When Simon Peter saw the Lord in the judgment hall he **surrendered with repentance,** *"And he went out, and wept bitterly" (Matthew 26:75).* A change in perception means a change in the person! Much like the church of the Laodiceans today's church need their eyes anointed with eyesalve *(see Revelation 3:18).* Many of our problems are vision problems.

Through the prophet Isaiah we get a fresh **vision of His Person**. Isaiah's eye had been diverted from a dead king below to a divine King above! He saw one before whom the host of heaven would not walk or upon whom they would not gaze. This was because of the purity of His nature. The whole earth was filled with His glory. At sound of His voice the posts of the doors moved and the house was filled with smoke. There was none like Him in all of heaven or earth! With a view of His loftiness Isaiah perceived his lowliness. How could he stand much less speak to such a one as this? Have we been slain by His person?

Hosea the prophet gives us a **vision of His Purchase**. Like the unfaithful wife of Hosea whom the prophet bought back, God has purchased us off of the auction block of sin. He paid the supreme sacrifice when He gave His Son a ransom for our sins. *"But God commendeth his love toward us, in that, while we were yet sinners, Christ died for us" (Romans 5:8). "Forasmuch as ye know that ye were not redeemed with corruptible things, as silver and gold, from your vain conversation received by tradition from your fathers; But with the precious blood of Christ, as of a lamb without blemish and without spot" (I Peter 1:18-19).* If you are a recipient of God's grace you are now His purchased possession! You are no longer your own! God has taken occupancy of His purchased possession and expects to receive glory from it *(I Corinthians 6:19-20)*. We need a fresh vision of the **splendor of Calvary**, the **sinfulness of the creature**, and the **supremacy of the cost** God was willing to pay. How could any of us desire to do anything but that which pleases such a loving and sacrificial God as our God?

The prophet Jeremiah projects for us a **vision of His Position**. Jeremiah was told to go down to the potter's house. There God would cause Jeremiah to hear His words. Jeremiah watched as the potter wrought a work on the wheel. He watched, as that potter carried out his will over the will of the clay. Then God said, *"O house of Israel, cannot I do with you as this potter? . . . Behold, as the clay is in the potter's hand, so are ye in mine hand, O house of Israel" (Jeremiah 18:6).* Why do we think we have a right to usurp our will over the will of our Maker? God asked this question, *"Shall the clay say to him that fashioneth it, What makest thou?" (Isaiah 45:9).* Some act as if God were the creation of man rather than man being the creation of God.

How had Simon come to realize that Jesus was more than some religious figure of his day, but rather the one that is the appointee over and the commander? The revelation came only after hearing His word. *"And he sat down, and taught the people out of the ship. Now when he had left speaking, he said unto Simon" (Luke 5:3-4).* Could it be that the reason we know so little of the person, position, and purchase of Jesus is because we are neglecting His Word? When speaking to the rebellious Jews of His day, Jesus said, *"Search the scriptures; for in them ye think ye have eternal life: and they are they which testify of me" (John 5:39).* The word *"testify"* means to give evidence, obtain a good honest report, to witness. To neglect the Word of God is to cast aside the greatest record of fact about God.

Knowing that Jesus Christ was his Master, appointee over and commander, made it easier to respond in obedience to the command to *"Launch out into the deep, and let down your nets for a draught" (Luke 5:4).*

(II) The Word of Obedience – *vs.5 nevertheless*

Once Simon had heard the command to launch out there was an immediate conflict that arose within him, *"Master, we have toiled all the night."* Is this not the case with each of us when we hear the commands? The reason for this is because of the warfare between the Spirit and the flesh. Paul wrote in *Romans 8:7, "Because the carnal mind is enmity against God: for it is not subject to the law of God, neither indeed can be."* The word *"enmity"* means hostility by implying reason for opposition. The flesh does not want to yield and become subservient to the Spirit.

Even in the face of conflict Simon submits in obedience to God's will, *"nevertheless at thy word I will."* Simon Peter uses a very interesting word, *"nevertheless."* It means in spite of that. When the flesh objected to God's commands and began to present the case as to why not, Simon said, "in spite of that I will." In spite of **past failures** I will let down the net. *"Master, we have toiled all the night, and have taken nothing."* Simon Peter is thinking to himself, "the only thing I successfully did last night was to fail at catching fish and He wants to try it again." Last night's failure has only added to the burden of today. Simon Peter's clean net has become a **soiled net** and would now require the strenuous task of washing. The continuous labor involved in a night of fishing had left Simon with **sore muscles**. Simon had not recovered from the previous failure and Jesus wants a repeat performance.

In spite of **present objections** Simon Peter was willing to put the net into the water. Everything Simon Peter knew about fishing objected to *"Launch out into the deep, and let down your nets for a draught."* Peter was only one in a long line of family fishermen. He had been raised to do nothing but fish and his life depended on his expertise in fishing. Everything he knew about fishing objected to the **timing**. You don't fish on the Sea of Galilee in the daytime. Night is when you can escape the heat of the sun. It is at night that the baitfish move into shallow water and the bigger fish follow. Have you ever found yourself questioning God's timing in your life? The children of Israel found themselves standing on the shores of the Jordan River a second time. The first generation had died in the wilderness and it was time to occupy the Promised Land. There was only one problem, at this time every year the river overflows its banks and becomes impossible to cross *(see Joshua 3:15)*. It was not so much the task but the timing that God appeared to be mistaken about. God knows when the timing is right for each of us!

All of Peter's training objected to the **place**, *"Launch out into the deep."* Have you ever been guilty of saying; "While it might be possible over there, it can't be done here?" No self-respecting fish is going to swim into a net when it could escape by swimming under the net. If there is to be any chance of catching a fish, we have to change locations! The children of Israel were not so much in doubt of provision as it was the place. *"Yea, they spake against God; they said, Can God furnish a table in the wilderness?" (Psalm 78:19)*. Do you doubt the place that God has chosen for you?

Being from a fishing family, Peter had heard some pretty extraordinary tales about good fishing trips. He might have been privileged to have had some good trips and had caught a lot of fish but, he objected to the **task** before him, *"let down your nets for a draught."* Does Jesus expect us to go to the wrong place at the wrong time and catch *"a draught"* of fish? The word *"draught"* means a haul of fish. Jesus is not asking for one fish, a few fish, or even some fish, but a haul of fish. Have you ever felt like God had given you a task beyond your talents, abilities, and resources? This is how the disciples felt when Jesus told them to feed those five thousand men and their families. Philip told the Lord that two hundred pennyworth of bread would not be enough to give every person even a little. Then Andrew said,

"There is a lad here, which hath five barley loaves, and two small fishes: but what are they among so many?" (John 6:9). Just as our Lord accomplished the task through His disciples, He can do the same through you and me.

Pondering the command given him by Jesus, Peter felt that the chances for failure far out weighed those of success. Yet, in spite of **personal understanding** Peter would let down the net. For some reason we have come up with the idea that we must understand the command as well as the outcome in order to be obedient to God's commands. Such is not the case. When there was no more wine to be dispersed at the marriage in Cana of Galilee, Mary turned to the servants and said, *"Whatsoever he saith unto you, do it" (John 2:5).* The only thing any of us need to know in being obedient to the commands is the fact that they are truly His commands. If it is He that has spoken to us we have but one responsibility, obey! It is God's responsibility to take care of the results.

While we are not sure, Peter could have objected because of **possible embarrassment**. If he did what Jesus told him to do, he would look like the biggest fool in the entire country. Everybody knows this is not going to work and I have to live with these folks. What will my family and my friends think? Do we not find ourselves in a constant battle with the great enemy of embarrassment? It proves to beset all of us, but especially young people. We call it peer pressure. The fear of embarrassment affects our witness, our walk, and the performance of God's will in our lives. In spite of embarrassment I will let down the net.

In spite of past failures, present objections, personal understanding, and possible embarrassment, Peter put the net in the water. Peter settled the conquest with commitment. *"At thy word I will."*

(III) The Results of Obedience – *vs. 6-8*

Peter found out that obedience to God's commands always yields positive results! Obedience brings blessings. Water was turned to wine as servants responded to the command to fill and distribute. Eyes that were darkened from birth received their sight when the man was obedient to the command, go and wash. A fish yielded from its mouth sufficient silver to pay taxes as Peter responded to the command, cast in a hook. The widow redeemed her sons and received a living from a pot of oil when she was obedient to the command; *"borrow thee vessels abroad of all thy neighbours, even empty vessels; borrow not a few" (II Kings 4:3).* In response to the commands of God, a rod has become a serpent, water has come from a rock, the sea has been parted and the river held back. Obedience has brought life out of death, cleansing to a leper, and victory to the army of Israel. Obedience opens the windows of heaven!

When Peter put the net into the water there were **physical results**, *"And when they had this done, they enclosed a great multitude of fishes: and their net brake" (Luke 5:6).* On the heels of Peter's **actions** was God's **abundance**! When the net hit the water, there were more than **mere results**. There was more than one or two fish in the net. I say this respectfully, but any amount was more than Peter had taken that night and would have certainly been a blessing! God did not sprinkle a few crumbs on Simon's plate. He filled the net! May we ever be mindful of the fact that anything we receive is by grace and not merit. James tells us that, *"Every good gift and every perfect gift is from above, and cometh down from the Father of lights, with whom is no variableness, neither shadow of turning" (James 1:17).* Many have become foundered on the bountiful blessings of God causing them to become unthankful in their hearts and barren in their praise. Let us remember the admonishment of the Psalmist; *"Let every thing that hath breath praise the LORD. Praise ye the LORD" (Psalm 150:6).*

What God did was more than **minimal results**; *"they enclosed a great multitude of fishes."* The results were more than what could be expected by the average fisherman on any given day of fishing. Don't miss the two words that Doctor Luke used to describe what God had just done. There was a *"multitude"* of fish in the net! The word means a fullness, a large number or populace. Can you imagine the excitement in Simon Peter's heart as he feels the weight of the fish in the net? He has not even pulled it up out of the water and he knows there is plenty. The second word is *"great"* which means much in any respect or far passed. The net contained more than a large number, it contained far past what one could have expected the net to contain. Is this not what God told Jeremiah He would do? *"Call unto me, and I will answer thee, and show thee great and mighty things, which thou knowest not" (Jeremiah 33:3).* Paul described our God as one that *"is able to do exceeding abundantly above all that we ask or think" (Ephesians 3:20).* God told Peter to launch out into the deep for a haul of fish and God was true to His Word. The writer of Hebrews tells us that it is impossible for God to lie *(Hebrews 6:18).* He will always be true to His Word.

God gave **miraculous results**, *"and their net brake . . . And they came, and filled both the ships, so that they began to sink" (Luke 5:6-7).* What had just happened super exceeded anything that human talent or ability could do! With one broken net these men received from God enough fish to fill two ships to the point of sinking because of overfilling. There is no answer to the how but God! It had to be a miracle! This would not be the last time Simon Peter would see results like this. Entering into a town Jesus saw a fig tree and was hungry. When He found the tree to be barren, He said, *"Let no fruit grow on thee henceforward for ever" (Matthew 21:19).* What were the results of Jesus' words? *"And presently the fig tree withered away."* When the disciples saw it, they marveled. How does one get these kinds of results? Jesus' answer was, *"If ye have faith, and doubt not" (Matthew 21:21).*

The results of Peter's great multitude of fish were more than physical, there were **spiritual results,** which is the chief end of all God's blessings. When the water was turned to wine the spiritual results were, *"This beginning of miracles did Jesus in Cana of Galilee, and manifested forth his glory; and his disciples believed on him" (John 2:11).* God received the glory and the hearts of the disciples were established in faith. Peter's fishing trip would prove to be no different. There would be spiritual ramifications in Simon Peter's life because of the physical results. There would be the **revelation** of Jesus' nature. *"When Simon Peter saw it, he fell down . . . saying . . . O Lord" (Luke 5:8).* After Peter had heard the words of Jesus, he called Him Master, but after seeing His power, he called Him Lord. Jesus was not just the appointee over, but He was the supreme in authority. This was God in the flesh.

The results brought about a **repentant** spirit in Simon Peter, *"he fell down at Jesus' knees, saying, Depart from me; for I am a sinful man."* Peter saw himself vile and wicked before a Holy God. When he used the word *"man"* Peter saw his **depraved nature**. It was the nature he had acquired through Adam. Using the word *"sinful"* it speaks of his **despicable nature**, which was manifested by his actions.

With this kind of spirit and sight, it produces a greater **response** in Peter's life as God calls him to a higher spiritual plane. *"Fear not; from henceforth thou shalt catch men" (Luke 5:10).* Which can only be accomplished by **relinquishing** more of self, *"And when they had brought their ships to land, they forsook all, and followed him" (Luke 5:11).* This is a picture of spiritual growth and maturity in the life of God's child.

While there are physical results to being obedient to God's commands, let's not get hung up on these things for they are to generate spiritual results in not only our lives, but also the lives of those about us. If we will be obedient to the commands of God, blessings will follow and our faith will be seen. Faith has only one strategy when it becomes knowledgeable of God's Word, obey! Jesus said, *"And why call ye me, Lord, Lord, and do not the things which I say?" (Luke 6:46)*. True faith gives more than lip service, it responds with an obedient life.

Chapter Five

The Stifling of Faith

Hebrews 4:2 "For unto us was the gospel preached, as well as unto them: but the word preached did not profit them, not being mixed with faith in them that heard it."
Matthew 8:26 "And he saith unto them, Why are ye fearful, O ye of little faith? Then he arose, and rebuked the winds and the sea; and there was a great calm."

Webster defines stifle as to suffocate or smother, to suppress or check, to stop, and to die from lack of air. While it would be a blessing to tell you that all sinners are surrendering in faith to Christ and all saints are being strengthened in faith, it would be a lie for many are stifling faith. In lives where faith could flourish and show itself mighty, it is being suffocated, suppressed, checked and killed. This sad commentary is not limited to just the sinner, but is readily true in the life of many of God's children. In *Hebrews 4*, Paul uses an Old Testament account of the children of Israel's failure to enter the Promised Land to project the New Testament truth of faithlessness. Israel failed to enter because they did not appropriate faith just as many fail to **enter into the rest** of salvation because they do not appropriate faith. Others fail to **enjoy the rest** of salvation because of stifled faith.

Paul tells us that all were **exposed** to the same **witness**, *"unto us was the gospel preached, as well as unto them."* The entire group had been witnessed to by the means of preaching. All the people may not have had the witness of the same servant, but they had the witness of the same Spirit, the Holy Spirit. *"And when he is come, he will reprove the world of sin, and of righteousness, and of judgment" (John 16:8). "Howbeit when he, the Spirit of truth, is come, he will guide you into all truth:*

for he shall not speak of himself; but whatsoever he shall hear, that shall he speak: and he will show you things to come" (John 16:13). The Holy Spirit is witnessing to sinners and saints alike. There was **exposition** of the same **word**, *"but the word preached."* Both groups had the foundation upon which to build faith, the Word of God. They had all they needed for faith to flourish in their lives!

How is it possible for two groups to have the same witness of the same Word, and get different results? Paul said, *"the word . . . did not profit them."* It was not useful or beneficial to one group of hearers. Why was that? What they had received was *"not being mixed with faith."* Even though they had one part that was absolutely necessary which was the witness of the Word; they did not combine and commingle it with faith. Is this not what we see in the lives of numerous individuals? Within the congregation are several folks still under the condemnation of sin, bearing the burden of sin that will ultimately cause them to be cast into the lake of fire *(see Revelation 20:15).* They hear the same servant deliver the same Scripture, anointed by the same Spirit, yet there are different results. Some respond to God's invitation and receive eternal life and others remain in their sin. Why? *"For by grace are ye saved through faith" (Ephesians 2:8).* Some combined faith with the witness of the Word and it produced life; others do not!

When making reference to faith in the lives of men, even those that were redeemed, Jesus spoke of no faith, little faith, and great faith *(see Mark 4:40, Matthew 6:30 & 8:10).* Why is there such a large spectrum of faith in the lives of individuals? Faith can be suppressed as well as suffocated. In many lives faith is not strengthened, but rather choked and held in check. Paul said to one body of believers, *"Ye did run well; who did hinder you that ye should not obey the truth?" (Galatians 5:7).* Disobedience and being unresponsive to the truth was stifling their faith!

What can stifle faith in the life of an individual? The answers are so numerous that I have not the space nor ability to cover them all. I want to confine our study to three things that will stifle faith in the life of a sinner as well as a saint.

(I) Stifling Faith in the Sinner

When one considers the stifling of faith in the life of a sinner, that is one that still abides under the condemnation and wrath of a Holy God, it must be in the area of salvation. The first and foremost issue that must be settled in the life of a sinner is the matter of sin, that which alienates him from the family of God. This is an issue that all men must first address for all are sinners by nature. It is only after settling the sin question that one can consider faith in any other areas of one's life.

I want to look at three men that were confronted with the issue of salvation and their response. In each case faith was stifled as they turned from God's free gift to continue in their sin. The first is found in *Mark 10:17-23* and is referred to as the rich young ruler. If there was ever an individual that gave all indications of getting saved, it was this young man! Let's notice his **request**, *"And when he was gone forth into the way, there came one running, and kneeled to him, and asked him, Good Master, what shall I do that I may inherit eternal life?" (Mark 10:17).* The strength of his request is seen in the fact that he would not wait. The young man could not wait to see if Jesus would come to his side of town. Driven by a deep need, he not only seeks out the Lord, but makes haste to get to the Lord Jesus, *"there came one running."* This is a request that must be placed before the Lord today! The most impressive thing about this request was the subject, *"what shall I do that I may inherit eternal life?"* Jesus was consistently being bombarded by requests. The blind asked to be healed. The mother of James and John asked if her two sons could be given the prominent seats beside Jesus in the Kingdom *(see Matthew 20:21).* One individual felt like he was being treated unfairly by his brother in the matter of the inheritance and ask Jesus to intercede in his behalf *(see Luke*

12:13). This young man did not appear to be interested in any of these things. His request was for *"eternal life."*

This young man displayed **respect** when approaching the Lord Jesus, *"there came one running, and kneeled to him."* Unlike the scribes and Pharisees, this man had not come to challenge the Lord's position, but rather submit and acknowledge Him as Potentate. It is evident that the young man has received proper training at home and his social position has not caused him to forget his manners.

In addition to being trained in the social graces, he has been tutored in the scriptures. Jesus said to the young man, *"Thou knowest the commandments, Do not commit adultery, Do not kill, Do not steal, Do not bear false witness, Defraud not, Honour thy father and mother" (Mark 10:18).* From our Lord's testimony, it appears that this individual was well versed in the Law. It is necessary to remember that there is a big difference between aptitude and application! He was characterized as being **religious**. He had a head knowledge that manifested itself in pharisaical actions but not a heart knowledge that is revealed by attitude.

When he addresses our Lord we become aware of his **reverence**, *"Good Master".* The word *"master"* was an honorable term for those that taught or instructed others. This reveals a reverence of the Lord's position, when coupled with the word *"good"* it denotes reverence for His person.

This young man seems to have everything going for him. Surely he will be part of the heavenly host. That is what one would think until we hear our Lord say, *"One thing thou lackest" (Mark 10:21).* The word *"lackest"* means to be inferior, to fall short, to be destitute or suffer need. It was not a lot of things or even a few things that would keep this young man from exercising saving faith in the Lord Jesus Christ; it was just one thing. Faith would be stifled by a **foolish love**. While he wanted to go to heaven, he did not want to turn lose of the world, *"And he was sad at that saying, and went away grieved: for he had great possessions" (Mark 10:22).* When speaking to His disciples about this foolish love for the world, He said, *"How hardly shall they that have riches enter into the kingdom of God!" (Mark 10:23).* This young man would throw away the treasures of the eternal for the trinkets of the temporal. When I think of this young man I think of the countless souls that will die and go to hell off of a church pew. They have had all the benefits of training and tutoring. They are basically good people that cannot turn lose of the world and love God supremely. They lack the "one thing" needed to become a recipient of eternal life.

We find our second individual in *Luke 7*, his name is Simon and he was a Pharisee. Simon has called for the social elite and the spiritually enlightened to gather at his house for a meal. Jesus has been invited to join this prestigious group. We are not told how long Jesus had been there, but in the course of the meal, a woman from off the streets and known for her open sin came in and fell at Jesus' feet. She would enter a sinner and exit a saint. By an act of faith she would bear her burden of sin to Jesus and exchange it for splendor of salvation. Jesus said unto the woman, *"Thy faith hath saved thee; go in peace" (Luke 7:50).* Simon and the sinful woman are present at the same meal, in the presence of the same Master, hearing the same message, and one was liberated while the other remains lost. She stimulated her faith and he suffocated his faith. Simon's faith was stifled by a **fleshly loftiness**. When it came to salvation, Simon considered her too bad to get it and him too good to need it.

This loftiness can be seen in Simon's **attitude toward others**. With the exception of a chosen few, Simon perceived himself as being better than most. He possessed the attitude of the Apostle Paul prior to his conversion. *"Though I might also have confidence in the flesh. If any other man thinketh that he hath whereof he might trust in the flesh, I more: Circumcised the eighth day, of the stock of Israel, of the tribe of Benjamin, an*

56

Hebrew of the Hebrews; as touching the law, a Pharisee; Concerning zeal, persecuting the church; touching the righteousness which is in the law, blameless" (Philippians 3:4-6). What Paul considered a righteous diadem became repulsive dung when he saw himself as God saw him. Simon measured everyone by his own self-righteous yardstick.

Simon's loftiness can be seen in his **actions toward Christ**. There were Simon's internal thoughts, *"he spake within himself, saying, This man, if he were a prophet" (Luke 7:39).* Simon sat in judgment as he scrutinized every move of the Lord Jesus. He failed to understand that Simon would have to measure up to the standard of the Sovereign and not the Saviour measure up to Simon's standards. Jesus said in *John 5:22, "For the Father judgeth no man, but hath committed all judgment unto the Son."* Paul said, *"For we must all appear before the judgment seat of Christ" (II Corinthians 5:22).* Simon had failed to acknowledge our Lord's person or His position. Simon also withheld external treasures from the Lord Jesus. Jesus points out that Simon gave Him no water, no kiss, and no oil. While it does not say so, it is most likely that the other guests received these things. All of these things were nothing more than common courtesy. These were the things that would be extended to those that one respected and looked forward to having in their home. We sense that Simon's motives for inviting Jesus were anything but honorable.

Revealing Simon's **affections toward Jesus** would tell of the loftiness within Simon's heart. Jesus would reveal this defect in Simon by the means of a parable *(see vs. 41-43).* Jesus would tell of two debtors, two debits, and two acts of forgiveness, which yield two qualities of love. Great forgiveness of a great debit produces great love. Jesus was telling Simon that this vile, repulsive sinner loved Him far more than he did. The wicked woman loved the Saviour and Simon loved himself. Simon's attitude toward Christ effected his affections toward Christ, which determined his actions toward Christ.

Faith would not be activated in the life of Simon because he saw himself righteous before God. Because Simon only saw his good and never his guilt, he would stifle faith and seal his eternal destiny.

Our last individual is a man by the name of King Agrippa. He is a member of a tribunal that the Apostle Paul must appear before *(see Acts 25:22-24)*. For fear of injustices in the lower courts, Paul appeals for an appearance before Augustus. Festus has examined Paul and found him innocent of any crimes worthy of death. He would have released him except for the fact that Paul had appealed to Augustus. Festus must send a list of crimes with Paul and can find none. *"But when I found that he had committed nothing worthy of death, and that he himself hath appealed to Augustus, I have determined to send him. Of whom I have no certain thing to write unto my lord" (Acts 25:25-26).* After listening to Festus' testimony, King Agrippa desired to examine the Apostle Paul. In the process of examining a saint, King Agrippa was confronted with salvation. While looking for words to send to Augustus, he receives a word from God. King Agrippa was confronted by a **witness from the past** *(see Acts 26:1-3)*. Paul said to Agrippa, *"I know thee to be expert in all customs and questions which are among the Jews"* The customs that Paul is making reference to is not that of farming, industrial skills, or the basic manners of life, but rather, religious customs. Agrippa had knowledge of the Temple, the methods of sacrifice, and the God whom the Jews served. While Agrippa may have not had full discernment he would have had knowledge of the Passover lamb, the blood sacrifices, brazen altar, and the Jewish feast days. Each one of these was a type pointing to the perfect lamb that would be sacrificed for the sins of the whole world. Agrippa had knowledge of our Lord's death and the testimony of His resurrection. Every custom of the past was a witness testifying to the validity of Christ death, burial, and resurrection.

Agrippa was confronted by a **witness from Paul** *(see Acts 26:4-21)*. Building on the King's understanding of Jewish customs, Paul gives a personal testimony. Paul speaks of his **confidence** that was misplaced. Paul said of himself, *"of the most straitest sect of our religion I lived a Pharisee."* Being religiously lost, Paul put his confidence in the energy of the flesh. When he sought refuge in the law he found himself condemned. He tells of his acts of persecution, which speak of his **corruptness**. He had hatred for Christ, the Church, and for Christians. Paul then tells King Agrippa about his **crisis** on the road to Damascus when he is confronted by the one he has sought to destroy. But the crisis leads to **conversion** as Paul submits to the Lord Jesus Christ. Now all Paul wants to talk about is his **Christ**. He became so excited about his witnessing that he is accused of being mad.

The last witness to confront the King is a **witness from the prophets** *(see Acts 26:22-27)*. Paul delivers to Agrippa the Word of God. It is the Word that will clarify the witness of the past and give credibility to the witness of Paul. If the other witnesses do not line up with the Word, they are false. True faith can only stand upon the foundation of God's Word. Paul points out that Agrippa has not only received present knowledge of the Word, but has past knowledge of the Word. King Agrippa is not ignorant to the truth of God's Word.

Will the King accept the testimony of the three witnesses and submit to the Lord Jesus Christ as Saviour? Will he respond in faith? *"Then Agrippa said unto Paul, Almost thou persuadest me to be a Christian" (Acts 26:28)*. Faith was stifled by **faulty logic**. King Agrippa considered salvation a matter of the head and not the heart. *"Persuadest"* means to convince by argument, to assent to evidence or authority. It is *"with the heart man believeth unto righteousness; and with the mouth confession is made unto salvation" (Romans 10:10)*. The King would dismiss with his head the things he should embrace with his heart.

Love, loftiness, and logic would keep these three individuals from accepting Jesus Christ as their Saviour. While they had a witness and the Word, they did not add faith. Too much riches, too much righteousness, and too much reason stifled faith and sealed their eternal doom. Is this true of you?

(II) Stifling Faith in the Saint

It would delight me to be able to say that once an individual exercised faith in Christ as Saviour and was made a child of the King; they allowed faith to flourish in their lives. I cannot say that because it is not true from a personal aspect or from biblical examples. There have been times in my Christian journey that I have stifled faith. Turning from the leadership of the Spirit, and the scriptures, I sought the path of sight. While it grieves my heart to admit my weakness, I am sure it grieves the heart of God more. The display of weak and anemic faith in the life of the believer is a slam on the character of God. It calls into question His abilities, actions, and affections.

When God moved upon men to pen the Word of God, He did not hide the flaws of those we consider Bible heroes. He did not magnify their attributes and minimize their blunders. He did not make them inaccessible. When speaking of Elijah the Bible said, *"Elias was a man subject to like passions as we are" (James 5:17).* God recorded for us David's sin *(II Samuel 11:3-4)*, Elijah's shortcomings *(I Kings 19:4)*, Moses' spirit *(Numbers 20:10)*, and Peter's surrender *(Matthew 26:70)*. Why would God do such a thing? *"Now all these things happened unto them for ensamples: and they are written for our admonition, upon whom the ends of the world are come. Wherefore let him that thinketh he standeth take heed lest he fall" (I Corinthian 10:11-12).* The men and women of the Bible are to serve as tutors. We are to learn from them by applying the good and avoiding the bad.

With faith being such an important aspect of the Christian life, it is needful that we study the aspect of faith in the lives of some Bible characters. By seeing those things that strengthen as well as stifle faith, we can possibly avoid the same mistakes and duplicate the success. I want to draw your attention to three specific areas that will suffocate, suppress, and stop faith in the believer's life.

When we look at the life of a man by the name of Demas, faith is stifled by a **foolish love**. Paul is writing his second letter to young Timothy. In most of his other letters Paul closes with a list those that are with him and their salutations. This letter would be no different with the exception of listing not only those that were with him; he would list those that had left him. *"For Demas hath forsaken me, having loved this present world, and is departed unto Thessalonica; Crescens to Galatia, Titus unto Dalmatia" (II Timothy 4:10).* Paul does not feel it necessary to tell us why Crescens went to Galatia or Titus went to Dalmatia, but he does want us to know why Demas has departed to Thessalonica, *"having loved this present world."* The others may have left to serve, but Demas left to escape service. The others may have responded to the Sovereign's will, but Demas was motivated by self-will. I want us to see three things from this man's life.

Notice **where he went**, *"For Demas hath forsaken me . . . and is departed unto Thessalonica."* There are two problems that one must guard against when reading this text; reading too much into it and not reading enough into it. While that may not make sense to some, let me explain. As a preacher, I am prone to see more here than there is! I invision a person leaving the church, his family, and jumping into the cesspool of sin. After reading after several writers, most feel that this is not the case. He simply left Paul and went to Thessalonica. Paul did not say Demas was lost but rather Demas left! Demas left **commitment for commerce**. Oliver B. Greene said of Demas' move, "Thessalonica, a very prominent city in that day from the standpoint of commerce and trade; and probably he had become ambitious for riches and this world's goods." Demas had a shift in the things that were a priority in his life. He moved from ministry to money! Demas' previous commitment can be seen in the numerous times he is linked to Paul and Luke in the service of God. *"Luke, the beloved physician, and Demas, greet you" (Colossians 4:14). "Marcus, Aristarchus, Demas, Lucas, my fellowlabourers" (Philemon 1:24).* While he had not quit, Demas had cut back on his involvement in the work of God.

Demas had left a **companion for comfort**, *"Demas hath forsaken me."* When speaking of Luke, Demas, and himself, Paul spoke of being *"fellowlabourers."* Demas had been a co-laborer, a companion in labor, and a fellow helper. They had been buddies and it was all over. There had been times when they had wept together, suffered together, and rejoiced together. They knew each other's strengths, weaknesses, and dreams. The cord that they had that appeared to be so strong had now been severed by the love for another, *"this present world."* Demas has new friends, what's the big deal in that? Paul couldn't expect him to hang around this prison forever! He had done his part, it was time to go on with life!

Demas had left a **crown for convenience**, *"this present world."* Albert Barnes said of Demas' return to the world, "Having desired to remain in this world rather than go to the other." Demas had found it easier to yield to the desires of the flesh rather than fight them. With the flesh being dominate in his life, Demas thought little of the heavenly and mostly of the earthly. He did not contemplate on rewards in heaven but rather riches at home! While he would not admit it, Demas was throwing away the true riches of life. Harry Ironside said, "He was more concerned about temporal things than he was about getting a reward at the judgment-seat of Christ, and therefore his name goes down on the page of Holy Scripture as a warning to every servant of Christ." Listen to the warning of John the beloved in *II John 1:8, "Look to yourselves, that we lose not those things which we have wrought, but that we receive a full reward."* It was not that Demas would not have any rewards, just not as many!

I must be careful to not read too much into this text, but you must be careful and not read too little into the text. While Demas was not out of church, he was one step closer. While Demas was going to heaven, he was less prepared for it. While he may have not lost his family, he was not a light to those that were lost. The danger of backing off is quitting! For many the **commerce leads to corruption**. Soon one finds justification for their business practices. We find reasons for breaking the laws of God and call it good business. Sunday becomes like every other day. Our standards are dropped and things that we would have never done previously become just standard operating procedure. Our attitude becomes, "God understands, it's just the price one has to pay."

There is the danger of **comfort leading to callousness**. That tender spirit that looked for an opportunity to give to others is gone. You find yourself saying, "Let them work like I do for what they get!" "If they had used good judgment, they wouldn't have to have the church folks keep them up." Soon the increase of more only fuels the desire for more! One can become callous to the leadership of the Holy Spirit and is unmoved by the convicting power of the Holy Scriptures.

Soon **convenience leads to carnality**. If there was an appetite for the Word, it is for the milk of the Word, for the digestive system can no longer handle meat. This condition is justified by condemning others as being legalist. Soon we find ourselves saying, "Don't they know that we are no longer under the law, but we are free in Christ." That great preacher of grace, the Apostle Paul, said, *"For, brethren, ye have been called unto liberty; only use not liberty for an occasion to the flesh" (Galatians 5:13).* The Apostle Peter said, *"As free, and not using your liberty for a cloak of maliciousness" (I Peter 2:16).* Because the flesh dominates us, the lines of separation are erased. This leads to one having the appearance of the world as well as its appetite.

While Demas may have not gone far, he had gone far enough to get into trouble. When Demas left, we have no further record of him. We do not really know how far he went!

Let's look at **why he went,** *"having loved this present world."* Sometimes we try to make things harder than they really are. I have read numerous commentaries on *II Timothy 4:10* trying to come up with an elaborate answer as to why Demas left Paul and went to Thessalonica. No matter how you analyze it, slice it or dice it; the simple truth is he loved the world more than he loved the things of God. It may not be right and we may not want to admit that this is a problem for many of God's children, but a love for the world has pulled many an individual away into spiritual bankruptcy. Paul uses a descriptive term for the object of Demas' affections. Paul used the word *"present"* which means, present in time, now or immediate. Demas loved the continual reoccurring earthly things of the age in which he lived. He was perfectly content gratifying the hunger of the flesh and as long as the flesh dominated him there would be no change. Demas would only go back when his heart would lead him back!

Take a look at **what he did,** *"For Demas hath forsaken me . . . and is departed."* Until I began to study these verses carefully, I had not seen the devastation left in the wake of Demas' desertion. In order to justify our actions, we are prone to say, "I only hurt myself." How I wish that were true. In many instances, my thoughtless actions have hurt others far worse than me. I have seen the selfish acts of a parent adversely change the course of life in a youngster. Employees had closed businesses and subjected their employer to legal prosecution. World leaders have taken the countless lives of young men and women, destroyed families, and crushed a nation's economy by selfish acts.

Demas would do far more damage than just hurting himself! He **discouraged a comrade,** *"Demas hath forsaken me."* While

Demas would ultimately have an effect on those he did not know and would never meet, his actions discouraged a comrade. Ironside said, "He does not say that Demas has forsaken God, or given up his faith in the Lord Jesus Christ, but that *"Demas hath forsaken me."* One writer said it thus, "Left me behind in my trouble." At this time Paul was in his second imprisonment, while awaiting execution as a martyr for Christ's sake. Barnes said, "He simply made it plain that Demas had turned his back on him – that as the old apostle stood in the shadows of death, when he really needed friends and the encouragement friends could give, Demas forsook him." *"Forsaken,"* means to leave behind in some place or to desert. Like a soldier that had been wounded in the fierceness of the battle, Paul felt like his comrade had deserted him and left him to be subjected to more of the enemy's cruelty. The wounds of the enemy had taken its toll on the body, but the wounds he had received from his friend had destroyed his heart. This abandonment can be further seen in his cry for Timothy, *"Do thy diligence to come shortly unto me" "Do thy diligence to come before winter" (II Timothy 4:9&21).* Two times Paul uses the phrase *"Do thy diligence to come."* Paul wants Timothy to use speed and make every effort to get there as soon as possible! Paul felt like Demas had left him when he needed his companionship and comfort the most.

The actions of Demas had **devastated a cause**, *"Demas . . . is departed. Take Mark, and bring him with thee: for he is profitable" (II Timothy 4:10-11).* Demas was not willing to stay in the heat of the battle and subject himself to the possibilities of martyrdom so he left. Some would have you think that the departure of Demas was of little consequence to the work of God. This is not the case! Every one of God's children is important to the ministry. When Demas left, there was a vacancy in the ranks, a void that would need to be filled. This is why Paul tells Timothy to bring John Mark. Paul said, *"for he is profitable."* The word means easily used or useful. What a testimony to have! This was not always the case with John Mark. In *Acts 13*, John Mark had turned back to Jerusalem and abandoned the work. Later, his actions would cause such contention between Paul and Barnabas that they would separate *(see Acts 15:39)*. This was not the case now! John Mark had started out badly and ended well, while Demas had started out well and ended badly! Our slackness and self-will has a great effect on the work of God. It not only distracts from the cause, it can disrupt the cause.

If Demas' actions had not discouraged a comrade and devastated a cause, it would still be wrong for he **disobeyed a command**, *"Love not the world" (I John 2:15).* As an old man, John the beloved wrote these words, *"Love not the world, neither the things that are in the world. If any man love the world, the love of the Father is not in him. For all that is in the world, the lust of the flesh, and the lust of the eyes, and the pride of life, is not of the Father, but is of the world" (I John 2:15-16).* Demas was living in direct disobedience to the Word of God. He was displaying an uncharacteristic life style for a child of God. And he was failing to disperse the darkness with the glorious light of the gospel of Jesus Christ. If for no other reason than this, Demas cannot justify his course of actions.

Demas was no longer a vibrant Christian with a strong faith, but he was a worldly individual that was making little difference in a corrupt world. His faith had become stifled by a foolish love for the world he was to have lived in contrast to.

I want us to take a close look at Simon Peter. This would be the individual that would preach the main message on the day of Pentecost. Peter enjoyed great moments of fame, but there had also been times of shame! Being a natural leader all of the other disciples looked to him for guidance. A habit that was not always wise, *"Simon Peter saith unto them, I go a fishing. They say unto him, We also go with thee" (John 21:3).* It was a **fleshly loftiness** that stifled Peter's faith and caused him to be brought down to such a low ebb.

Simon's departure from the ministry followed his denial of the Master. *"Then began he to curse and to swear, saying, I know not the man" (Matthew 26:74).* Three times Peter is confronted with being associated with this man named Jesus. Giving an opportunity to stand and identify with Christ, Peter disavows any relationship with this man. Having been openly shamed before his Lord and Saviour, Peter runs off into the darkness weeping. Why had this man of strength and confidence failed so miserably? Peter's strength and confidence had been misplaced. Peter was resting upon the flesh! The Apostle Paul said, *"have no confidence in the flesh. Though I might also have confidence in the flesh. If any other man thinketh that he hath whereof he might trust in the flesh, I more" (Philippians 3:3-4).* Paul had a very impressive pedigree. Others would have trusted it, but Paul trashed it for confidence in God. An Old Testament writer said, *"For the LORD shall be thy confidence, and shall keep thy foot from being taken" (Proverbs 3:26).* We can have confidence in the Lord for supplication *(see I John 5:14)*, and stability *(see II Thessalonians 3:4)*, but never place any confidence in self.

Simon Peter's faith was smothered by a fleshly loftiness, which can be seen in his **superior view** of himself. The Lord tries to warn and prepare Simon Peter for the attack of Satan. *"And Jesus saith unto them, All ye shall be offended because of me this night: for it is written, I will smite the shepherd, and the sheep shall be scattered" (Mark 14:27).* Simon heard nothing! Looking to himself, Peter saw himself superior to **his companions**. Peter said, *"Although all . . . yet will not I" (Mark 14:29).* This warning may have been needful for the others, but not me! By making the assumption that he will succeed where others fail, is that not thinking one's self better than others? Has Peter not become a judge of his brethren? After encouraging us to *"Humble yourselves in the sight of the Lord, and he shall lift you up" (James 4:10),* James gives this solemn warning, *"who art thou that judgest another?" (James 4:12).* "Judgest" means to distinguish, decide, to try, or to call in question. This superior attitude is a sin against God and the brethren.

Peter's confidence caused him to see himself as being superior in **his commitment**, *"Although all shall be offended, yet will not I."* The word *"offended"* means to be tripped up, to entrap, and to entice to sin. Peter's superior attitude makes him a perfect candidate for being ensnared by sin. When writing to the Corinthian church, Paul tells them that the record of Israel's journey was for our benefit *(see I Corinthians 10:11)*. Their conduct and God's chastisement was to be a rebuke to our evil ways. Paul tells them that the very thing that they thought could not happen would happen if this warning were ignored. *"Wherefore let him that thinketh he standeth take heed lest he fall" (I Corinthians 10:12).* Peter ended up falling because he thought he couldn't and Paul didn't fall because he thought he would. *"lest that by any means, when I have preached to others, I myself should be a castaway" (I Corinthians 9:27).*

Confidence in the flesh caused Peter to view himself as being superior in **his courage**, *"But he spake the more vehemently, If I should die with thee, I will not deny thee in any wise" (Mark 14:31).* He had been confident of his superior commitment and his superiority to his companions, but he was even more confident of his courage! Mark used a very descriptive phrase to describe Peter's response when the Lord told Peter that he would deny the Saviour, *"more vehemently."* Peter was certain that he would not be moved in his commitment and he was resting in his superiority to others, even more settled than these were was his courage for the Lord. Peter had never backed down from a fight and tonight would be no different! How sad to find out that it was not the **waving of a sword**, but the **word of a servant** that brought his demise. There can be no confidence put in the arm of the flesh!

Simon Peter's faith was smothered by a fleshly loftiness, which can be attributed to his **scriptural void**, *"for it is written" (Mark 14:27).* Things are going to become very intense for all of the Lord's disciples. The followers of Christ were looking for the day of His coronation and not His crucifixion. The cross will shatter their hopes and dreams! In preparation for that day, Jesus begins to reveal the coming events. He does this with the Word of God. Jesus wanted to enlighten their spiritual understanding, but Peter rejected it. There were two areas we can see a scriptural void in Simon Peter's life.

There was a void when it came to the **recorded Word**. The Word that Jesus gave to the disciples that night was taken from the Old Testament cannon of scriptures. All that was about to happen had been prophesied by Zechariah, *"Awake, O sword, against my shepherd, and against the man that is my fellow, saith the LORD of hosts: smite the shepherd, and the sheep shall be scattered: and I will turn mine hand upon the little ones" (Zechariah 13:7)*. The Word had been there all the time! It would have helped prepare them for this moment of persecution, opposition, and tribulation. This scriptural void is not relegated to Simon Peter's life only. Countless numbers of God's people have been needlessly shipwrecked by the winds of adversity when it should not have happened. We have a recorded word of admonishment from one that has fallen to these strong winds. *"Beloved, think it not strange concerning the fiery trial which is to try you, as though some strange thing happened unto you" (I Peter 4:12)*. Contrary to much of what you hear, the Christian is not exempt from the adversities of life.

Peter experienced a void in hearing the **revealed Word**. The Word was not only recorded for Simon, but Jesus was now revealing that Word to him. Peter would not listen! God had a personal word for the disciples, yet they turned to a confidence in self rather than trusting the Scriptures. Is this truth not seen in the lives of each of us? God uses a servant, anointed by the Spirit, to deliver to us the Scriptures and we turn away from the truth. We find it easier to have confidence in the works of self than the Word of the Sovereign. I would tell you why that is, but I do not know why we are so foolish!

Simon Peter's faith was smothered by a fleshly loftiness, which leaves behind a **shattered victim**, *"And Peter said, Man, I know not what thou sayest . . . And the Lord turned, and looked upon Peter. And Peter remembered the word of the Lord . . . And Peter went out, and wept bitterly" (Luke 22:60-62).* While Peter had done what he said he would never do, he had done exactly what the Scriptures and the Saviour said he would do. Peter was now a broken man! Peter was now a man of **shame**. Peter had broken his word and God's Word. It would be bad enough when all the other disciples found out about his cursing accusation, *"Then began he to curse and to swear, saying, I know not the man" (Matthew 26:74),* but he would never get over that look upon the face of his Lord. If he could have found a rock, he would have crawled under it. This was something that he would never live down.

He must not only deal with the sense of shame, but **separation**, *"And Peter went out."* Though not separated from the family, he felt separated in the area of fellowship. Sin had gotten between him and the Lord that loved him so much. How could he ever approach the Lord Jesus in such a defiled state? While each of us knows that our God is a God of forgiveness and He moves toward the wayward to restore them, that aloneness is heartbreaking to the child of God.

The shame and separation led to **sorrow**, *"wept bitterly."* Peter did not slip away silently and lick his wounds, but the phrase implies to violently wail aloud. Peter had wanted to remain silent about the beloved, but this was not the case with the bitter results. Peter could not contain himself and neither did he try to! While Peter had found it distasteful to identify with Christ in the judgment hall, he made no effort to do so now. The snare of sin and the glance of the Saviour had broken his heart.

Peter's lofty spirit had made him a man of **surrender**, *"Simon Peter saith unto them, I go a fishing" (John 21:3).* Making a mess of things, Peter felt like the only thing to do is to quit. He had had some failures in the fishing business, but nothing like this blunder. Peter had not learned anything! In self-confidence, he had leaned on the arm of the flesh and by returning to the fishing business that was all he was doing, turning to something he thought he could do. Jesus did not let him succeed at that either, *"Then Jesus saith unto them, Children, have ye any meat? They answered him, No" (John 21:5).* God had a message and a ministry for Simon Peter and He would not let Peter be successful in anything else.

Like Peter, when one places confidence in self, trouble is not far away. Peter's fleshly loftiness stifled his faith just like it stifles the faith of all God's children. Look away from the "I" of self unto the great "I AM." In Him one will find a solid rock upon which to rest one's faith.

For our final thought on the stifling of faith in the life of a believer, we will once again look at an event in the life of Simon Peter. By considering another event in the life of Simon it serves to remind us that each of us can stifle faith in various ways. While there may be one dominate area of weakness in our faith, there are many more that may surface at any time! In *Matthew 14:22-36* Jesus constrained the disciples to get into a ship and go to the other side while He sent the multitude away. Soon the disciples would find themselves in a storm in the midst of the sea. In the fourth watch, Jesus comes walking on the water. Fearing Him to be a spirit, they begin to cry out when they hear Him say, *"Be of good cheer; it is I; be not afraid" (Matthew 14:27).* Peter's response to the Lord's words of comfort was, *"if it be thou, bid me come unto thee on the water" (Matthew 14:28).* Jesus simply tells Peter to *"come."* Getting out of the ship, Peter began to walk to Jesus until his faith was stifled and he began to sink. **Faulty logic** would stifle the faith that had gotten him out of the ship and begin his miraculous journey across the waves. Human reasoning kicked in and the waves soften under his feet. In response to his cry of distress, *"immediately Jesus stretched forth his hand, and caught him,* *and said unto him, O thou of little faith, wherefore didst thou doubt?" (Matthew 14:31).* **Operative faith** became **oppressed faith** when faulty human logic was injected into the situation. Logic told the wave walking Peter that he could not do what he was already doing, so he stopped walking on the water.

There are several things that permit faulty logic to stifle faith in the life of the believer. Faith was stifled by **logic's focus,** *"But when he saw the wind boisterous" (Matthew 14:30).* Faith focuses on the Sovereign and logic sees only the storm. Faith embraces Christ and logic is embraced by the circumstances! Logic causes the believer to focus on the wrong thing.

Peter is ensnared by **logic's fear,** *"he was afraid; and beginning to sink, he cried, saying, Lord, save me" (Matthew 14:30).* Fear chips away at the firm foundation of faith causing Peter to begin to sink. Fear and faith are mortal enemies. Each desires to make the other its servant and assert dominance over the other. Logic is on the side of fear!

The stifling of faith is accomplished by **logic's forgetfulness.** Logic causes the believer to forget "Him." Logic caused Simon Peter to forget all about the Lord Jesus while focusing on everything else. Faith says remember "Him" while logic says forget "Him." In this account there are several things that logic will not encourage Peter to remember.

Logic forgets about **His prayers,** *"he went up into a mountain apart to pray" (Matthew 14:23).* In the midst of the storm, Jesus was in the midst of supplication. He was praying for each one of them. Logic never reminds us that, *"he ever liveth to make intercession for them" (Hebrews 7:25).* The Lord Jesus was in prayer because of **His perception,** *"the ship was now in the midst of the sea, tossed with waves: for the wind was contrary" (Matthew 14:24).* There is not one thing about us or that will ever happen to us that He does not have total awareness of and total control over! Jesus saw every strike of the oar and sensed every anxiety that streaked through their spirit. He is a God that cares!

Soon the disciples would experience **His presence**, *"And in the fourth watch of the night Jesus went unto them, walking on the sea" (Matthew 14:25).* Logic distracts the believer from the conscious awareness of the Lord. *"For he hath said, I will never leave thee, nor forsake thee. So that we may boldly say, The Lord is my helper, and I will not fear" (Hebrews 13:5-6).* He is there all the time! Peter needed to remember **His power**, *"walking on the sea" (Matthew 14:25).* That very day Peter had witnessed the Lord's power over **substance** as He multiplied the loaves and fishes. If Peter would but focus on Christ he could see His power over the **storm** as Jesus stood there upon the waves.

Logic would not encourage Peter to rest in **His promise**, *if it be thou, bid me come unto thee on the water. And he said, Come"* *Matthew 14:28-29).* Peter had gotten out of the boat in response to the words of Jesus. Peter was in obedience to the spoken word. God's Word could be trusted; Peter had proven it on numerous occasions.

The faulty logic of Simon Peter would cause him to turn away from the Lord in fear and forget the God of faith. The marvelous journey of faith across the waves would be stifled by faulty logic. Success would end in surrender as fear conquered his faith.

Whether it be the entering of rest for the sinner or the enjoyment of rest for the saint; faith is the appropriated means of entrance. The same elements of foolish love, fleshly loftiness, and faulty logic; will stifle faith in the lives of sinners and saints alike. Faith will liberate the soul of the sinner and bear the spirit of the saint into the heavenly realm. We have His Word, but we must mix it with faith.

Chapter Six

The Strengthening of Faith

Mark 9:23-24 "Jesus said unto him, If thou canst believe, all things are possible to him that believeth. And straightway the father of the child cried out, and said with tears, Lord, I believe; help thou mine unbelief."

In studying this man's faith there are some precious and priceless truths that need to be grasped. This man's faith must flourish in the **tragedy** of the valley rather than the **triumph** of the transfiguration. He did not dwell on the **mountain of enlightenment** with Peter, James and John, but sojourned in the **misery of evil** with a faithless generation. Faith is not designed to get you to the mountain, but bring the mountain into your valley. The songwriter said it so well, "The God of the mountain is still God of the valley." C.H. Spurgeon said, "A little faith will bring your soul to heaven; a great faith will bring heaven to your soul." May we take comfort in the words spoken to the disciples by the men in white apparel, *"this same Jesus" (Acts 1:11)*. The same Jesus that had communed with Moses and Elias on the mountain would converse with man in the valley. The same Jesus that was **transfigured in splendor** on the mountain would **triumph over sickness** in the valley.

In this story there would be two great feats. Listen to the words of J.D. Jones, "There are in effect in this paragraph the stories of two miracles. The first and most obvious is our Lord's triumph over the evil spirit. The second is not so obvious, but it is in many ways more wonderful still. Jesus not only drove the evil spirit out of the boy, but He won a triumph for faith in the soul of his father." Jesus was not only interested in the sickness of the son, but in strengthening the saint. Ron Dunn said, "That faith can and should grow is evidence from the use of such phrases as *'little faith'* and *'great faith.'* " Just as Paul longed to see a strengthening and maturing of faith among the Corinthian saints *(see II Corinthians 10:15)*, God desires growth in each of us.

(I) The Rival of Faith

Sometimes we are too hasty in responding to questions! You might be asked, "Would you like more patience?" While most of us could readily use a double portion of what we have, we generally forget what it takes to develop a good crop of patience, *"knowing that tribulation worketh patience" (Romans 5:3).* The best fertilizer for a good crop of patience is pressure, affliction, anguish, burdens, and persecution. While each of us desire more patience, none of us want the tribulation, yet it will require the one to produce the other. How would you respond if I were to ask you, "Do you want to strengthen your faith?" I hope you would say yes, but faith requires the same fertilizer as patience! While Abraham may have the faith to leave a **land**, to develop more faith would require offering a **lad**. Faith would cause the disciples to leave the **shore**, but for more faith Peter would have to leave the **ship**. If this man is to see his faith strengthened, there must be a rival. Something must challenge faith!

There was the rival of his **expectant faith**. When this man left home with his demon possessed son, he expected to return with a healthy son. That is what he expected! The whole purpose for making the journey was for one and only one reason, the healing of his son. We are not told a lot about this father. We can assume that he had heard that Jesus had performed great acts of healing. If this were not true what was he basing his expectant faith on? While he may have heard something, we have no assurance that he had ever seen someone healed or even personally knew someone that had enjoyed the touch of the Great Physician. Yet there was an element of faith drawing him to Christ with expectancy. His expectant faith was first challenged by **abandonment**. The father gets to where he thinks Jesus is supposed to be and there is no Jesus. Some of Jesus' disciples are there but Jesus has taken three of them into a mountain and no one has any idea when He will be returning. Things are not going the way he planned them. In his mind, this man knew how things were supposed to work. Has your faith ever become frustrated because things were not happening like you planned them, where you planned them and when you planned them?

Feeling bewildered this man turns to those he perceives as being closest to Christ. They had been there when Jesus multiplied the loaves and fishes. They have seen the lame walk, the dumb to speak, the blind see; they must have picked up enough to help his son. There is the rival of **ability** that has risen up to challenge his expectant faith. The disciples were not up to the task. Listen to what the man told the Lord, *"I spake to thy disciples that they should cast him out; and they could not" (Mark 9:18).* Has your faith ever been crushed under the heel of disappointment when those you perceived as super saints lacked the ability to solve your problem or lighten your load? You just knew they could help!

If things were not bad enough, this father must then face the **accusations** of others. *"And when he came . . . he saw a great multitude about them, and the scribes questioning with them" (Mark 9:14).* These scribes challenged every word and work of Christ and now they were critical of this man's act of faith. He began to ask himself, "Had I been so foolish to believe the words that I heard and expect God to do a supernatural act and heal my boy?" "What was I thinking when I left the house with such a silly notion?" Have you ever had others lavish you with a critical spirit of unbelief?

Expectant faith was drawing its last few breaths when Jesus came from the mountain to the valley. If faith could just hold on there would not only be the **transformation of the Saviour**; there would be a **transformation in the situation**.

The most difficult part of the strengthening of faith did not occur when the father's expectant faith was challenged, but the real battle would be the rival of his **existing faith**. While it may have seemed foolish to think God would supernaturally heal his boy, he was now caused to question the soundness of even believing in Christ at all. It is bad enough to watch the materials of new faith go up in smoke, but to have someone or something try to crack the foundation of your existing faith that's even worst! It was foolish to think the boy could be healed, but am I an even a bigger fool for believing at all?

It was Simon's existing faith that was challenged by Satan in *Luke 22:31, "Simon, Simon, behold, Satan hath desired to have you, that he may sift you as wheat."* It was the Psalmist existing faith that was questioned when he got his eyes upon the treasures with which the wicked indulged. *"But as for me, my feet were almost gone; my steps had well nigh slipped. For I was envious at the foolish, when I saw the prosperity of the wicked" (Psalm 73:2-3).* The rival of existing faith is a must in the growth process of faith! If the expectant faith was to be built, the foundation of faith must be proven to be sound and sufficient to hold the new structure.

The depth to which this challenge went can be seen in the words of this demonic son's father, *"if thou canst do any thing, have compassion on us, and help us" (Mark 9:22).* There would be a test in the man's existing faith in God's **ability**, *"if thou canst do any thing."* This would challenge the existing faith of God's **affections**, *"have compassion on us."* Lastly, the situation would rival the existing faith of God's **actions**, *"help us."* Can you not see this process being worked out in our own life? When faced with serious tribulation do you find faith in God's ability, God's affections and God's actions being challenged in your own heart?

A true champion can only be crowned and his talent appreciated after the successful rout over a worthy opponent. Peter said it thus, *"That the trial of your faith, being much more precious than of gold that perisheth, though it be tried with fire, might be found unto praise and honour and glory at the appearing of Jesus Christ" (I Peter 1:7).*

(II) The Refining of Faith

If our faith is to be strengthened it must be challenged. Most of us want to see our faith grow and mature, but we shy away from the confrontation of faith. One of the reasons for avoiding anything that rivals our faith is we do not like the refining process. None of us like having our faults and weaknesses exposed, especially in the area of spiritual matters. Yet, God designs life with many smelting furnaces for the express purpose of refining our faith that it *"might be found unto praise and honour and glory at the appearing of Jesus Christ" (I Peter 1:7).* Such was the case of this father with a demon possessed son.

There would be the refining of **faith's patience**. For most of us there is a little phrase that we do not like to hear, "you'll have to wait." Can you not identify with the man who said, "I want patience and I want them right now!" Motivated by parental love this impetuous father longs to see the demon vanquished and the child liberated from oppression. What ever it takes, the boy must be cured! The quality of the father's patience can be seen in his actions. When Jesus returns from the Mount of Transfiguration He finds a great crowd gathered about His disciples questioning them. Seeing Jesus the people run to Him and salute Him. Jesus asked what it was that they were questioning the disciples about. The answer was the immediate response of the boy's father, *"I have brought unto thee my son, which hath a dumb spirit" (Mark 9:17).* Please note to whom the man said he had brought his son, *"unto thee."* When the father left the house that day he had an expectant faith of getting his son to Jesus. The father goes on to say, *"I spake to thy disciples that they should cast him out; and they could not" (Mark 9:18).* Why had not the father waited patiently for the Lord's return? The father's hyper activity had not allocated a cure but generated great confusion. Sometimes our activity is a deterrent to our faith! Jesus wanted both the father and the disciples to learn about **faith's conformation**. After casting out the demon, Jesus and His disciples went into a house. There the disciples asked Him why their efforts had proven futile. *"And he said unto them, This kind can come forth by nothing, but by prayer and fasting" (Mark 9:29).* Prayer and fasting is a time-consuming process. It requires waiting on God for a confirmation of **His presence** and **His promise**. The presence of peace in one's heart would be the confirmation that God had heard everything and that He was responding with an answer. Unlike the wicked one, God does not like for His children to be anxious or filled with fright. Therefore, He has made it possible to have peace in the midst of the storm. If the disciples and the child's father had prayed and waited before the Lord, God could have sent the confirmation of peace thus enjoying now what others would receive later. If we were to pause and reflect on the entire story we would realize that the healing of the boy happened when it should have happened! The healing arrived when Jesus came on the scene and not before! The father and the disciples could have waited in peace rather than embarking on religious activity that only generated **anxiety in the saints** and **accusations by the scribes**.

In this waiting process the father would learn something of **faith's cure**. I think I could safely say that things were not developing in the exact way this father had planned them. He had not perceived Jesus' absence, the disciples' failure, the scribes' assaults, and the endless questions of Jesus. It would have been so simple if things had been done the way he had worked them out in his mind! Get up and go to Jesus. A quick touch by Jesus or a few words and home by supper time. For many this is their perception of faith. The mentality of today's religious world is grab the magic lamp of faith, give it a few quick religious rubs and some 'genie-jesus' pops up with three wishes. There are two things that I would like you to notice when the father finally got to Jesus. It appears that Jesus was in no real hurry to give relief to the father's stressful situation. Jesus converses with the father about the length of the illness, the magnitude of the illness, and the symptoms of this illness. I can imagine the father saying to himself, "just heal my son, we can talk about all these things later." The cure does not always occur when we think it ought. Secondly, in the process of talking with Jesus the situation appears to worsen rather than improve. The demon throws the boy to the ground and the lad begins to wallow and foam at the mouth. If that's not bad enough, when Jesus does rebuke the spirit it rent him sore and the lad appeared to be dead. Can you imagine what is going through the mind of the father as well as the multitude? Jesus was supposed to help us rather than hurt us! While the lad may have been tormented, at least he was alive! When Jesus intervenes in our behalf, things may appear to get worse before they get better. Mature faith does not give up! It is patience in spite of the timing of the cure. Mature faith does not wait for peace in the midst of the storm, but waits in peace!

In Jesus' conversation with this boy's father, we are permitted to see the refining of **faith's process**. When I make reference to faith's process, I am in no way implying a one, two, three, method that yields super faith. Rather, I am saying that there are certain elements found within the manifestation of true biblical faith. While there are many things that could be brought out about the process of faith, there are two that are very prevalent within the text before us. There is the refining of the **responsibility of faith**. The father turns to Jesus saying, *"if thou canst do any thing" (Mark 9:22).* Jesus responds to the parental plea *"If thou canst believe, all things are possible to him that believeth" (Mark 9:23).* The process of faith reveals that it is not a question of can Jesus, but can the father? It is not our responsibility to manufacture faith, but it is our responsibility to appropriate the faith given us. Paul said, *"I am crucified with Christ: nevertheless I live; yet not I, but Christ liveth in me: and the life which I now live in the flesh I live by the faith of the Son of God, who loved me, and gave himself for me" (Galatians 2:20).* When speaking of faith the writer of *Hebrews* said, *"Looking unto Jesus the author and finisher of our faith"*

(Hebrews 12:2). If there was a weak link in the boy's healing it was not Christ. Jesus said to the father, *"If thou canst believe."* The key that would open the lock and liberate his son from demon oppression was the father's faith. Listen to what Jesus said to the woman with the issue of blood. *"Daughter, thy faith hath made thee whole; go in peace, and be whole of thy plague" (Mark 5:34)*. Two blind men followed Jesus through the streets and into a house crying out for mercy. Jesus asked them if they believed that He was able to heal them? In response to an affirmative answer Jesus said, *"According to your faith be it unto you" (Matthew 9:29)*. Whether it is the need of salvation or substance the individual is responsible for appropriating faith. This truth can be seen in the following example. *"For unto us was the gospel preached, as well as unto them: but the word preached did not profit them, not being mixed with faith in them that heard it. For we which have believed do enter into rest" (Hebrews 4:2-3)*. If those that heard the gospel were to enter into rest, their hearing must be combined with faith. Without faith the hearing of the gospel would not be useful or of any benefit to them. The Lord was able to bless the father and his son if the father was able to believe.

There is the refining of the **resources of faith**. Look at the father's plea in contrast to Jesus' response. The father said, *"if thou canst do any thing" (Mark 9:22)* and Jesus said, *"If thou canst believe, all things are possible to him that believeth" (Mark 9:23)*. Jesus wanted this man to realize that his vision was too small. What the man cried for was far smaller than the resources made available to him through faith. The father's plea reveals that he would settle for *"anything"* and Jesus is trying to get him to understand the resources of faith are *"all things."* Paul knew this truth when he said with a confident faith, *"I can do all things through Christ which strengtheneth me" (Philippians 4:13)*. God is no miser, but rather He delights in abundantly blessing His children. We are encouraged to approach the throne with confidence, *"Let us therefore come boldly unto the throne of grace, that we may obtain mercy, and* *find grace to help in time of need" (Hebrews 4:16).* We are also encouraged by the words of the Apostle Paul in *Romans 8:32, "He that spared not his own Son, but delivered him up for us all, how shall he not with him also freely give us all things?"* We are not approaching God as beggars, but rather believers. God is not in the business of allocating scraps, but rather opening the storehouse. Fear will keep you on your hands and knees under the table while faith will give you a seat at the table. Just remember that the *"anything"* on the floor first came from the *"all things"* on the table!

As Jesus converses with this troubled father, He is orchestrating events to refine the father's faith. Maturity will come to faith's patience and faith's process. When Jesus finishes the father and the son will have been blessed.

(III) The Reviving of Faith

It is not God's purpose to **stifle** this man's faith, but **strengthen** it! While it may appear at first that the process will end in **death**, its final scene is **deliverance**. True biblical faith would deliver the father from **fear**, the son from **feebleness**, and the disciples from **failure**. It is not the desire of Jesus to damage faith, but develop faith! The father was eaten up with dread, the son with disease and the disciples with doubt. All this would change when Jesus got through strengthening their faith.

God is interested in establishing a true biblical faith in all of His children. The strengthening process of faith is an endless one. Just as we grow in Him, we grow in our ability to believe Him. Faith can only be replaced by sight! Until then each of us must allow God to orchestrate events in our lives so that we might mature and develop daily. The mature biblical faith that God desires in each of us is a faith that touches every aspect of man: body, soul, and spirit.

As this story of faith closes, Jesus departs and passes through Galilee *(see vs. 30).* In the wake are three lives that have been changed because faith has been strengthened. The son has experienced a **healing**. For many today there is a fear attached to a testimony of someone being healed of some disease that has corrupted their lives and destroyed their health. When the word healing is mentioned many individuals are beset with negative connotations. They envision healing lines and a religious showman merchandising the Holy things of God. They see healing as a charade fueled by emotion and ignorance. While this reaction may partly be justified because of the abundance of religious shysters feasting upon the weakness of others, many simply are fearful of the supernatural acts of God. Their inability to explain what has happened causes them to reject the experience of healing. Somewhere between emotionalism and intellectualism, there is the Biblical truth about healing. Healing is still in the Bible and God still heals! *"Is any sick among you? let him call for the elders of the church; and let them pray over him, anointing him with oil in the name of the Lord: And the prayer of faith shall save the sick, and the Lord shall raise him up" (James 5:14-15).* God has provided a means and a method of healing. A strengthened faith yielded the healing of this young man's body!

Faith not only touched the boy's body, but the father's soul. Faith had lifted the burden that this father bore. Heaviness had been replaced with **happiness**. It would be an understatement to say that the return home was more jovial than the journey there! The seat of this man's emotions had been touched as true Biblical faith was strengthened to embrace the fullness of God's power. A **worshipful spirit** had replaced a **woeful spirit**. We are only permitted to view the strengthening of this man's faith from the completed story. Who would not be happy if their son had been liberated from demon oppression and divinely touched by the Master's hand. If we are to understand the truth about mature faith there is a question we must consider. When was this man's disposition changed from that morning to merriment? We are not specifically told! What we are not permitted to know in practice, we are knowledgeable of in principle. If it occurred after the boy's healing then there was no real change in this area of the man's faith life. It requires no faith to rejoice after the blessing has materialized. Biblical faith is not hindsight but rather foresight. Faith embraced a healed son while he was yet being rent sorely and cast to the ground as dead. Would not what you knew in your heart cause you to rejoice as much as what you would later see with your eyes? Faith would embrace the promise before the hands could embrace the person. If the father's faith had flourished peace had replaced panic previous to the actual act of healing. Faith replaces the torment before the treatment is administered! Faith changes you in the midst of circumstances. This principle of faith is seen in the life of the Apostle Paul when the messenger of Satan buffets him *(See II Corinthians 12:7-10)*. When by faith Paul embraced the promise of sufficient grace to meet the need the emotional makeup of Paul changes. *"Therefore I take pleasure in infirmities, in reproaches, in necessities, in persecutions, in distresses for Christ's sake" (II Corinthians 12:10)*. Faith can cause you to experience the sunshine in the midst of the storm. Mature faith touches the soul of man and generates peace in the midst of the storm.

The disciple would gain **hope** from this faith experience. When Jesus arrives on the scene there is a state of bewilderment among the people. There is an air of criticism within the scribes, and the disciples have been spiritually wounded by failure. While the disciples had some concern about healing the boy's body and their emotions were grieved by their inabilities, their biggest concern was spiritual. They needed a strengthening of faith that would touch their spirit! This was not their first attempt at ministering to the needs of others. They had been dispatched with power and authority previous to the death of John the Baptist. *"And they went out, and preached that men should repent. And they cast out many devils, and anointed with oil many that were sick, and healed them" (Mark 6:12-13)*. After burying the body of John the disciples gathered with Jesus to tell of their many mighty works *(see Mark 6:30)*. Their **previous**

feats had been crushed and relegated to a place of insignificance by their **present failure**. The disciples had been wounded in their spirit. There would be two areas from which help would come to strengthen their faith and touch their spirit. Hope would begin to germinate from the **acts of Jesus**. *"But Jesus took him by the hand, and lifted him up; and he arose" (Mark 9:27)*. If Jesus had been unable to heal this boy and demonstrate His authority over all spirits then the disciples knew that they were doomed for a life of defeat. This was not the case! By His mighty hand, Jesus had silenced the critics, liberated a life, encouraged a father and gave hope to His disciples. They had received His power and authority earlier. Why would they not be given it again? Were not the works of the Master to be the works of His men?

When they arrived at the house the disciples would be encouraged by the **answer of Jesus**. *"And when he was come into the house, his disciples asked him privately, Why could not we cast him out? And he said unto them, This kind can come forth by nothing, but by prayer and fasting." (Mark 9:28-29)*. While they were concentrating on why they couldn't do it, He was telling them how they could do it. Note how our Lord worded His response to the disciples, *"This kind can come forth."* In another instructional session with His disciples He said to them, *"Verily, verily, I say unto you, He that believeth on me, the works that I do shall he do also; and greater works than these shall he do; because I go unto my Father" (John 14:12)*. After the healing of this young lad the disciples would have their spirit touched.

True Biblical faith is not unbalanced faith, but touches every aspect of man. Because man consisted of a body, soul, and spirit God has a complete faith for the complete man. This father with some faith brings his boy to Christ for healing. Christ is totally knowledgeable that there is a need in the life of the father as well as the son. He thus orchestrates the events of life so that He can care for the boy's sickness and **strengthen** the father's faith.

Chapter Seven

The Sovereignty of Faith

Mark 1:40 "And there came a leper to him, beseeching him, and kneeling down to him, and saying unto him, If thou wilt, thou canst make me clean."

Leprosy is one of the most vicious and ruthless diseases ever to befall the human race. Jerry Vines said, "A leper was a walking death that lasted an average of nine years until its victim finally collapsed in a pile of corruption." It was a disease that not only had physical ramification, but also inflicted social rejection. E.W.G. Masterman said, "No other disease reduces a human being for so many years to so hideous a wreck." It is in this wretched state that we find a man of great faith. With total disregard for the law, this leprous man races to the feet of Jesus. My heart is caused to leap for joy as I hear the words of faith, *"If thou wilt, thou canst make me clean."* While this man knew firsthand the **cruelty of the disease**, he was comforted in knowing the **compassion of the Divine**. Exceeding the knowledge of many, this man's comfort was not contingent on receiving a cure or being relieved of his circumstances! It is evidenced by his approach that the leper desired healing, but that is not his chief end. Peace is not so much in being **cured**, but in **conforming**. The greatness of this man's faith has caused him to seek the **will of the Creator** over the **wellness of the creature**. A.B. Simpson pointed out that we are to lay down our own will in submission to the will of God. We are to have a will in harmony with His will. This is exactly what this poor leper has done! In the turbulence of this storm of sickness this individual found peace in the **sovereignty of faith**.

(I) The Shadows of Sovereignty – "If"

Are you continually plagued by your limited knowledge of events and find yourself asking repeatedly, "What is God doing?" Don't be too discouraged; most of us are plagued by the same experiences. While there are many aspects of God's will and ways that are recorded for us in His precious Word, much of the means by which these things will be accomplished are hidden. Every child of God has been given the precious promise of heaven, *"In my Father's house are many mansions: if it were not so, I would have told you. I go to prepare a place for you. And if I go and prepare a place for you, I will come again, and receive you unto myself; that where I am, there ye may be also" (John 14:2-3).* The **substance** of the promise is God's Word; the **shadow** of the promise is we do not know if it will be by means of the rapture or by way of the grave that we attain heaven. This is the very reason God has equipped us with faith. Faith allows us to peacefully stand in the shadows and embrace the substance of the promise.

When the leper approaches the Lord Jesus Christ, he said *"If."* This word is a conditional particle with the idea of, in case that. It is often used in connection with other particles to denote indefiniteness or uncertainty. The glorious truth is that the *"if"* only has application to the leper and not the Lord. While the leper may be looking at the shadows of God's will, the Lord is looking at the substance of His will! There is no uncertainty or indefiniteness when it comes to God.

The writer of the letter to the Hebrews said, *"Neither is there any creature that is not manifest in his sight: but all things are naked and opened unto the eyes of him with whom we have to do" (Hebrews 4:13).* There are two phrases that I want to draw your attention to in this text, *"any creature"* and *"all things."* The first means, the thing such as a building, creation, creature, or ordinance. The second means, the whole and implies whatsoever and whosoever. There is not one thing, past, present, or future that has happened, is happening, or will happen that He is not fully aware of! One old preacher put it this way, "Has it ever occurred to you that nothing has ever occurred to God?" There are no "ifs" with the Sovereign, only with His subjects!

I believe that this leper was contented with the shadows, as we too should be. There is a comfort that comes with the shadow of sovereignty. A shadow can only be generated by light shining upon substance. The light must not only shine on it, but it must be behind it if we are to stand in the shadow. God is not standing in the light, but He is the light *(see I John 1:5)*. Every one of our shadows is nothing more than substance, which God is behind! Whatever He is behind, it will be for our good and for His glory. *"And we know that all things work together for good to them that love God, to them who are the called according to his purpose" (Romans 8:28).* The shadow of Sovereignty is caused when "The Light" stands behind the substance of His will!

Almost every day I find myself bewildered by the turn of events in my life or the lives of those about me. It may be the death of a child or the tragedy of a car wreck. There may be the gift of life at the expense of another in childbirth. It would be futile to try to list all the things we question about life for the list would be endless! But, bewilderment does not have to fester and become bitterness. The germ that leads to the devastating epidemics of doubt, bitterness, and despair is known as "why." Why do bad things happen to good people? The truth is I do not know, but He does. While that may not comfort you, it is a comfort to me. I am comforted in the fact that it is enough just knowing that He has full knowledge and control of all things. *"For as the heavens are higher than the earth, so are my ways higher than your ways, and my thoughts than your thoughts" (Isaiah 55:9). "O the depth of the riches both of the wisdom and knowledge of God! how unsearchable are his judgments, and his ways past finding out" (Romans 11:33)!* This one thing I know, when I cannot **trace His hand**, I can **trust His heart**! *"For as the heaven is high above the earth, so great is his mercy toward them that fear him" (Psalm 103:11).* In most cases, I do not know the answer to why. The greater truth is, it is not necessary for me to know why! It is not **facts** that have generated peace in this leper's heart; it is **faith**. Faith is the only thing that can disinfect the circumstances of life from the germs of why and enhance spiritual well being.

(II) The Sovereign of Sovereignty – *"thou"*

As I read the leper's statement of faith, I sense within it an air of confidence. The confidence is not within self because he is perplexed by *"if."* The leper's confidence is in the person he has knelt before, the Lord Jesus Christ. He is the Sovereign of Sovereignty! Like that leper, each of us can make our way to Jesus with full assurance. We can have confidence in **who He is**. This unnamed leper has approached more than a mere man; he has bowed in submission to the **Creator**. The one before whom this leper has fallen was the one that formed him in the womb of his mother. It is He that breathed the breath of life into man and man became a living soul *(see Genesis 2:7)*. It is in Him that we live and move and have our being *(see Acts 17:28)*. This Jesus is the source of all things! *"For by him were all things created, that are in heaven, and that are in earth, visible and invisible, whether they be thrones, or dominions, or principalities, or powers: all things were created by him, and for him: And he is before all things, and by him all things consist" (Colossians 1:16-17)*. If there is to be a change in the leper's situation, his Creator will be the one to do it!

The leper has come to the **Christ**. When Jesus asked His disciples who He was, Peter responded with *"Thou art the Christ, the Son of the living God" (Matthew 16:16)*. There before the leper's eyes was God in the flesh. This was not just a god of the many gods' this was the one true and living God! This was the God of whom Moses and the prophets had spoken. Before him was the Living Word, *"In the beginning was the Word, and the Word was with God, and the Word was God. The same was in the beginning with God" (John 1:1-2)*.

This troubled soul has bowed before the **Coming King**. While others may choose to wait, this humble creature bows in recognition of our Lord's rule. There is a day coming when all will submit and confess Him as Lord of Lords and King of Kings. *"For it is written, As I live, saith the Lord, every knee shall bow to me, and every tongue shall confess to God" (Romans 14:11)*. The Father has given Him all power. We are told that the government shall be upon His shoulders and all things placed under His feet *(see Isaiah 9:6, Ephesians 1:22)*. Our Lord shall rule with unrivaled power and authority!

The one before whom this diseased creature has fallen is more than mortal man. This is his **maker**, his **master**, and his **monarch**! It is in peace that he awaits the will of his Lord.

The Leper has approached the Lord Jesus with confidence in **what He is**! Within this statement of faith, there is no uncertainty cast upon the person of the one the leper has bowed before. Why? One might ask. There can be no uncertainty because there is no uncertainty when it comes to God's **character**, *"For I am the LORD, I change not" (Malachi 3:6)*. Two elements of God's character are light and love. *"This then is the message which we have heard of him, and declare unto you, that God is light, and in him is no darkness at all" (I John 1:5)*. *"And we have known and believed the love that God hath to us. God is love; and he that dwelleth in love dwelleth in God, and God in him" (I John 4:16)*. This leper knows that his God will not respond to him or his need with hatred or evil. What has happened in his life and is yet to happen is tempered by love and light!

There is no uncertainty in God's **commands**. *"For all the promises of God in him are yea, and in him Amen" (II Corinthians 1:20)* *"For ever, O LORD, thy word is settled in heaven" (Psalm 119:89)*. When this man made his request unto the Lord he did not know what words Jesus would utter, but he was certain of one thing. What ever He said, it would come to pass! All things are upheld by the word of His power *(see Hebrews 1:3)*. It was by His word that the heavens were made and the worlds were framed *(see Psalm 33:6, Hebrews 11:3)*. At His command the sea was calm, sight was given, and sickness was vanquished.

Confidence can be placed in the certainty of God's **course**. While it may appear to many that there is no rhyme or reason to the course of human events, this leper knows that the divine plan of God is being carried out to the letter. For those that know the True and Living God, the words luck and chance can be removed from their vocabulary. This man rests in peace knowing that the determinate council of God is at work in his life and what ever happened would be according to that plan. This man has only a limited understanding of the past events in his life and is totally unaware of the future. Yet, he knows one that has complete knowledge of the end from the beginning because He determined it! While he may not know the details of that course, he knows they will be right because of the character of the one that has designed it. *"Shall not the Judge of all the earth do right?" (Genesis 18:25)* His ways are not only loftier than our ways, but they are holier.

There is no uncertainty in His **control**. This leper was confident of God's character; God's commands, God's course, but also God's control. This needy creature was in total agreement with the words of Job, *"But he is in one mind, and who can turn him? and what his soul desireth, even that he doeth. For he performeth the thing that is appointed for me: and many such things are with him" (Job 23:13-14)*. It does not matter what arises to challenge or deter that divine plan, God's council will be carried out.

Knowledgeable of the person to whom he had brought his petition, this leper waits in peace. His greatest desire is to **exalt the Sovereign** and not so much **eliminate the sickness**. He simply wants his will to conform to the will of God. Because of who He is and what He is, the answer to his petition will be right!

(III) The Strategy of Sovereignty – *"wilt"*

When this individual makes this great statement of faith, *"If thou wilt, thou canst make me clean"*, it is apparent that he has full confidence in the **ability** of the Lord even if he does not know the **answer** of the Lord. While he does not know the answer, he knows the nature of the answer. The answer will be in harmony with the perfect will of God. The more I study the statement this man made, the more impressed I am with his spiritual wisdom and insight. He was aware that there was a strategy to sovereignty. Webster defines strategy as the art or science of conducting a military campaign in its large-scale and long-term aspects. It is the skill in achieving a purpose. This leper knew that God's will consisted of actions and events that would achieve the large-scale and long-term purposes of God. This truth is seen in the word *"wilt."* It means to determine as an act, an alternative to an impulse, to choose or prefer by implying to wish, to be inclined to.

From the word *"wilt"* we can see the **timing of sovereignty**. The large-scale and long-term purposes of God are a determined act. Sovereignty is not **reactive**, but rather **resolve**. God is not waiting to see the course of events so He can plan His next move. God is not reacting to things as they develop; His acts are already determined. Not only is God's Word forever settled; but also so are God's works, God's ways, and God's will! This leper is not requesting God to make a decision about his healing for he is aware of the fact that the decision has been made. The peace of God is not in **altering** God's will but **aligning** with God's will. This truth is seen in the life of the Lord Jesus. Jesus said, *"For I came down from heaven, not to do mine own will, but the will of him that sent me" (John 6:38)*. In the garden the Son rested in the will to the Father when He said, *"not my will, but thine, be done" (Luke 22:42)*. God has already determined His response to every act or situation placed before Him by any created being. God never has asked Himself, "What am I going to do?" I am glad that God cannot be surprised by anything or anybody. While life may catch me off guard and leave me perplexed, this will never happen to our Heavenly Father! Our God is immutable and never indecisive. He is in total control!

This leper takes comfort in the **temperament of sovereignty**. The purposes of God are not impulsive acts driven by sentiment. While few of us like to admit it, I have allowed my feelings to cloud my better judgment on numerous occasions. Moved by sentiment I have hurt individuals as well as myself. We can find an example of harmful sentiment in the acts of nature. A chicken will lay eggs and set on them for a prescribed number of days at which point the chicks will begin to emerge from the egg. The chick will begin to peck a hole in the shell and struggle to free itself from what appears to be a coffin. Moved by sentiment, many have stepped into the process trying to help liberate the chick only to kill it. It is in the struggle that life is given. The chick is attached to the egg sack and only at the appointed time can it be liberated from it. A premature break brings death to the chick. The motive of the person was that of **help**, but it proved only to be an act of **harm**! God is not swayed by emotion. While God is a God of love, His love will never pervert His judgment! His love may temper but never destroy His divine purpose! Let me use an illustration I once heard. A little boy was playing out in the yard with his older sister. It was in the summer and he was running barefoot across the yard when he stepped on a briar. He immediately began to cry because of the thorn embedded in his little foot. Coming to his aid his mother got some alcohol and a needle and proceeded to remove the thorn from her child's foot. His response was even more crying and screaming. It was then that his sister stepped up and said, "Mommy will not hurt you any more than it takes to help you." The purpose of the mother was not to harm, but rather help her child. Her heart was touched by the anguish and pain she witnessed in the life of her small child, but she must not allow sentiment to keep her from doing what is best for the child. We are blessed by this divine truth,

"For we have not an high priest which cannot be touched with the feeling of our infirmities" (Hebrews 4:15). Our God is not without feelings and He can identify with our pain, but it will never cloud His judgment nor deter His eternal purpose. We will never be harmed by the love that God has for each of us. Unlike earthly parents, our Heavenly Father will not discard divine principles and purposes under the pretense of something we call love, but will carry out that, which is best for the child because of love. Ron Dunn said, "I am reluctant to say this because it is something I'd rather not hear and something I do not want to acknowledge, but the greatest works God has done in my life, He has done against my pleasure – and against my will."

Within the statement of faith we can see the **tactics of sovereignty**. Remember the definition of strategy, the art or science of conducting a military campaign in its large-scale and long-term aspects, the skill of achieving a purpose. One can come to a hasty conclusion when one prejudges the outcome of the war when viewing a single skirmish. What one needs to keep in view is the purpose, the final objective. The great commander is looking at the big picture, which is made up of numerous segments. This leper was not viewing things from a **disease in life**, but rather the **duration** and **destination of life**. It is not in one blow of the hammer that the sculpture is created, but by numerous and varied processes administered by the artist. The true appreciation of an artist can only come after seeing the final product! What appears to be a fatal flaw in the process of forming the sculpture may very well be that single act that makes the artist great and the work extraordinary. Satan would like to convince each of us that one aspect of our development could be skipped and the outcome is the same. This is not true! There are no shortcuts in God's developmental processes. This divine truth can be seen in the life of Joseph. It was only after the pit, Potiphar's house, and the prison that he was ready for the palace. Only then could he say, *"But as for you, ye thought evil against me; but God meant it unto good, to bring to pass, as it is this day, to save much people alive" (Genesis 50:20)*.

God has an ultimate purpose that has been determined. In the accomplishment of that predetermined purpose there are various stages and processes that must occur. The leper rests in the assurance that God does all things well.

(IV) The Strength of Sovereignty – *"canst"*

The leper did not say that there was a possibility that Jesus might be able to heal him, he said, *"thou canst make me clean."* The word *"canst,"* means to be able, can do, and be of power. If this leper must live the rest of his life, what ever that may be tormented by the merciless disease of leprosy it would be because of **providence** and not the absence of **power**. When speaking of the Lord Jesus, Paul said, *"Now unto him that is able to do exceeding abundantly above all that we ask or think, according to the power that worketh in us" (Ephesians 3:20).* The word *"able"* in this verse is the same Greek word as *"canst"* in our text. There is no weakness in God! Paul tells us that God's power is exceeding, above and beyond. It is super abundant in quantity, superior in quality, and excessive. Man has never exhausted God's power nor has fathomed its depth. Paul said it exceeds your asking or your thinking.

His power is **adequate for His purposes**. What ever God has determined to do, He has the power to do it and nothing can hinder it! Job's face to face encounter with God yielded this affirmation of God's power. *"But he is in one mind, and who can turn him? and what his soul desireth, even that he doeth. For he performeth the thing that is appointed for me: and many such things are with him" (Job 23:13-14).* God sends word for Jeremiah to go down to the potter's house. There Jeremiah watched as the potter wrought a work on the wheel. He was permitted to watch the entire developmental process and at the conclusion was told to ask His people Israel this question. *"O house of Israel, cannot I do with you as this potter? saith the LORD. Behold, as the clay is in the potter's hand, so are ye in mine hand, O house of Israel" (Jeremiah 18:6).* His power is not limited in the **manifestation** of His purpose or the **methods** of accomplishing them. *"The LORD hath his way in the whirlwind and in the storm, and the clouds are the dust of his feet. He rebuketh the sea, and maketh it dry, and drieth up all the rivers: Bashan languisheth, and Carmel, and the flower of Lebanon languisheth" (Nahum 1:3-4).* He has power over all things. Jesus said in *Matthew 28:18, "All power is given unto me in heaven and in earth."*

God's power is **appropriated in His promises**. Of His own will God has made that power available to the household of faith. Jeremiah was given this promise of power, *"Call unto me, and I will answer thee, and show thee great and mighty things, which thou knowest not" (Jeremiah 33:3).* God has promised to respond to the cry of His child with a demonstration of His power that would supersede anything they had known. In the New Testament we find power promised unto the believer. In *Acts 1:8*; we are promised power for the purpose of being a **witness**. *"But ye shall receive power, after that the Holy Ghost is come upon you: and ye shall be witnesses unto me both in Jerusalem, and in all Judaea, and in Samaria, and unto the uttermost part of the earth."* The disciples were promised power for greater **works**. *"Verily, verily, I say unto you, He that believeth on me, the works that I do shall he do also; and greater works than these shall he do; because I go unto my Father" (John 14:12).* There is sufficient power for our earthly **walk**. *"According as his divine power hath given unto us all things that pertain unto life and godliness, through the knowledge of him that hath called us to glory and virtue: Whereby are given unto us exceeding great and precious promises: that by these ye might be partakers of the divine nature, having escaped the corruption that is in the world through lust" (II Peter 1:3-4).* God has promised the child of God His power. Through the indwelling of the Holy Spirit divine power would be appropriated and available to all.

That same power that liberated the sinner and brought to pass all His divine purposes will be **allocated for His punishment**. *"The LORD is slow to anger, and great in power, and will not at all acquit the wicked" (Nahum 1:3)*. Paul said in *Hebrews 2:3 & 10:31, "How shall we escape, if we neglect so great salvation."* *"It is a fearful thing to fall into the hands of the living God" (Hebrews 10:31)*. There is an appointed time when all principalities and powers will submit to Him. They will fall prostrate at His feet and *"every tongue should confess that Jesus Christ is Lord, to the glory of God the Father" (Philippians 2:11)*. They will then be cast in to the lake of fire to be punished for all of eternity! There are none who will be able to stand in opposition to Him.

Approaching the Lord Jesus Christ this man of faith said, *"thou canst."* There was no region beyond the reach of His power. There was no creature that could resist His power and situation that could not be resolved by His power. There was sufficient strength in the Lord to do all things whatsoever He will!

(V) The Submission to Sovereignty – *"make me clean"*

This poor leper has come to the Lord Jesus Christ believing that God has sufficient power to cleanse, purge or purify his body of this terrible disease. This man desires to be made clean, but does not usurp his will over the Sovereign's will. As one reads the entire account, the atmosphere of submission marks it. The gentle creature yields to the wisdom of his Creator. There are at least three areas that we can see submission in the life of this leper. The individual projects a **submissive spirit** in his approach to the Saviour, *"And there came a leper to him, beseeching him."* The word *"beseeching"* means to call near, invoke by imploration, to intreat. Total control of the situation is left in the hands of the Lord Jesus. This man has not come to force the hand of God but rather conform to the hand of God. The leper has come to ask of God and not to argue with God. He does not perceive himself as a rival council that must convince the divine jury of heaven to vote his way. He is fully aware of who is the servant and who is the Sovereign!

When this man enters the presence of Jesus, he demonstrates a **submissive stature**, *"kneeling down to him."* Taking his place at the feet of Jesus this man bows to the Lordship of Christ. Knowing peace could be found at the feet of the Saviour this man allows his outward actions to reflect his inward attitude. He has not come to confront his equal, but rather honor his superior.

In this man's statement of faith we can see a **submissive speech**, *"saying unto him."* The word *"saying"* is an interesting word. It means to lay forth or relate in words usually a systematic or set discourse. When this man said, *"If thou wilt, thou canst make me clean"*, these were not words that just came to mind the moment he met Jesus. This was a predetermined discourse that had been fashioned by one who desired God's will. The boundaries of the request were determined by what he knew of the character and nature of the one he would approach. What he had to say would honor the Creator and humble the creature. While he sought a purging, it must not nullify any praise due the Saviour.

In simple humility this leper comes to the Lord Jesus. Everything he says and does projects submission to the Sovereign. His confidence and peace is in knowing that God's will is best. While the **circumstances of life** may be dimmed by shadows, the **character of the Lord** is perfectly clear to him. Fully confident of his Lord's ways, he places himself upon the altar; body, soul, and spirit. The songwriter George Stebbins was right when he said, "Have Thine own way, Lord! Have Thine own way! Hold o'er my being Absolute sway! Fill with Thy Spirit Till all shall see Christ only, always, Living in me." Have you found peace in the sovereignty of the Saviour?

Chapter Eight

The Silence of Faith

Mark 12:43-44 "And he called unto him his disciples, and saith unto them, Verily I say unto you, That this poor widow hath cast more in, than all they which have cast into the treasury: For all they did cast in of their abundance; but she of her want did cast in all that she had, even all her living."
James 2:18 "Yea, a man may say, Thou hast faith, and I have works: show me thy faith without thy works, and I will show thee my faith by my works."

In addition to Mark's account, Doctor Luke also records for us the story of the little widow with the big offering. There are numerous Bible truths projected from this account and all worthy of our study but I want to confine our study to the **silence of faith**. I do not want to give the impression that faith does not speak, for faith has a great deal to say. Faith is vocal in one's **salvation**, *"That if thou shalt confess with thy mouth the Lord Jesus, and shalt believe in thine heart that God hath raised him from the dead, thou shalt be saved" (Romans 10:9).* Faith is vocal in the saint's **salutations**, *"Let the redeemed of the LORD say so, whom he hath redeemed from the hand of the enemy" (Psalm 107:2).* Faith is vocal in our surrender to **service**, *"I heard the voice of the Lord, saying, Whom shall I send, and who will go for us? Then said I, Here am I; send me" (Isaiah 6:8).* Faith speaks loud and clear when it is necessary. But, true faith manifests itself in the life as well as the lips! I once heard someone say, "What you're doing speaks so loud, I can't hear what you are saying." In the epistle of James, the writer points out that true biblical faith is not just a saying faith, but also a showing faith. Words minus works equal no faith!

While this poor widow's faith may appear to be silent to the ear, it speaks volumes to the eye. Jesus saw and heard it! The fanfare, the fortunes, and the flesh mesmerized the disciples, but not Jesus. While others had their eyes upon the festivities, Jesus was looking for faith. In the healing of the centurion's servant, some listened for the words of **commendation**, *"That he was worthy . . . For he loveth our nation, and he hath built us a synagogue" (Luke 7:4-5)*, Jesus looked for the works of faith, *"neither thought I myself worthy . . . but say in a word" (Luke 7:7)*. When the disciples listened to the mother's words of **cunning**, *"Truth, Lord: yet the dogs eat of the crumbs which fall from their masters' table" (Matthew 15:27)*, Jesus was looking for the works of faith, *"O woman, great is thy faith" (Matthew 15:28)*. When opening blinded eyes, others listened to words for **compassion**, *"Thou son of David, have mercy on us" (Matthew 9:27)*, Jesus looked for the works of faith, *"According to your faith be it unto you" (Matthew 9:29)*. In the healing of a son, the disciples listened to the words of **crisis**, *"if thou canst do any thing" (Mark 9:22)*, Jesus looked for the works of faith, *"Lord, I believe; help thou mine unbelief" (Mark 9:24)*. Jesus was looking for faith when others were listening for words. Where do you place the emphasis when you are looking for the substance of faith?

Luke asks an interesting question concerning our Lord's return, *"Nevertheless when the Son of man cometh, shall he find faith on the earth?" (Luke 18:8)*. While we cannot be sure of Christ finding faith upon His return, we are confident that He saw faith in this poor widow's life. This little lady projects for us the **silence of faith**.

(I) The Observer - *"And Jesus sat . . . and beheld"*
To the boisterous shouts of the people, *"Hosanna; Blessed is he that cometh in the name of the Lord" (Mark 11:9)*, Jesus made His entrance into Jerusalem on the back of a colt. He proceeds directly to the Temple where He was met by the religious opposition of the Sadducees and the Pharisees. Their motivation

for living was to criticize the works and curtail the ministry of Christ. *"And they send unto him certain of the Pharisees and of the Herodians, to catch him in his words" (Mark 12:13).* After silencing His attackers by exposing their ignorance to the truth and their conformity to tradition, Jesus blisters them with a woeful judgment *(see Mark 12:38-40).* He then turned and made His way to the court of the women.

Upon His arrival to the court of the women, Jesus began to observe. The actions of Jesus revealed the **practice** of the observer *"And Jesus . . . beheld" (Mark 12:41).* *"Beheld"* means to be a spectator, discern, or consider. The people were totally unaware of His presence or His practice; Jesus watched what was taking place in the courtyard. Have we forgotten that the Lord Jesus Christ is watching everything that is transpiring in the lives of men? Matthew used an interesting phrase three times in chapter six in reference to our alms, our prayers, and our fasting, *"thy Father, which seeth in secret" (vs. 4, 6, 18).* There is nothing that we can conceal, do in private or think inwardly that our Father does not observe! He has full knowledge of every aspect of what we say, do, or think. Job confidently said, *"But he knoweth the way that I take" (Job 23:10).* Our God is an observing God. This truth can also be seen in the day of judgment, *"And I saw the dead, small and great, stand before God; and the books were opened: and another book was opened, which is the book of life: and the dead were judged out of those things which were written in the books, according to their works" (Revelation 20:12).* Not only is God in the practice of observing, He is recording those things that He observes. We will one day face our true record recorded from a heavenly perspective!

We are also told something of the **position** of the observer, *"sat over against the treasury" (Mark 12:41).* J.D. Jones suggests that Jesus sat down on the steps leading to the court of the women. This being the case, He would have occupied a **clear position**. Jesus would have been able to see the entire courtyard.

There in the courtyard scattered among the columns were thirteen boxes called shopheroth or "trumpets." They were given this name because of their shape. Shaped like a trumpet, they had a narrow mouth or opening and gradually grew larger toward the bottom. They were placed there to receive the offerings of the worshippers for the support of the Temple. J.W. Shepard tells us that Mary, the mother of Jesus, would have placed the price of two turtledoves or two pigeons in the third of the thirteen trumpet-shaped collection boxes to redeem her first born from priestly service. The wording of the text also reinforces the fact that his view was unobstructed, *"over against."* The phrase *"over against"* means directly opposite. He did not set among, but rather directly opposite all thirteen boxes so He could see all. He enjoyed a **continual position** as He viewed the courtyard. The word *"sat"* means to set, to settle, dwell, continue, or tarry. Jesus did not take a quick glance and leave, but rather settled in for continual observation. Jesus is not some casual observer to the activities of men, but rather He forever is in the business of observing our activities.

Lastly, we want to take knowledge of the **perception** of this observer, *"the people."* The thought here is that Jesus saw a throng of people. He did not just see one here and one there, but He saw them all. From the richest aristocrat to the lowliest peasant, Jesus saw every one of them. There was not one that escaped the eye of our Lord Jesus Christ. The songwriter said, "His eye is on the sparrow, and I know He watches me." J.D. Jones said, "He has eyes not simply for men of great and outstanding powers and services, but also for those quiet, humble, lowly folk whom the world never notices, and who never get their names into the newspapers." When speaking of God's perception, David said, *"If I say, Surely the darkness shall cover me; even the night shall be light about me. Yea, the darkness hideth not from thee; but the night shineth as the day: the darkness and the light are both alike to thee" (Psalm 139:11-12).* I am always in His sight.

Just as Jesus sat and observed the courtyard of the women, He sits today observing the courtyard of the world. His eye is upon not only all men collectively, but all men individually. From the high-rises of the world's largest cities to a single grass hut in an obscure jungle on the Dark Continent, there are none that escape His sight. With a lofty position and total perception, our God is in the practice of observing all.

(II) The Observation – *"beheld how the people cast money into the treasury"*

Seated upon the steps, our Lord observed the activities of the people as they moved about in the courtyard of the women. Because of God's Word we can gain great insight into observation of the observer. Please notice something about the **subject of observation**. Perched upon the steps Jesus took the place of an observer, but He was not the only observer. There was many that day that had come to the Temple to observe. On one occasion the disciples took Jesus to the Temple for the purpose of seeing the physical structure, *"and his disciples came to him for to show him the buildings of the temple" (Matthew 24:1)*. Some had come to the temple to observe the festive giving of the rich. While it was not the case with all, the sounding of horns and a parade of servants would precede many of the wealthy givers. Elaborately dressed, the rich would follow their exposed gifts of flamboyance. While there were many that had come to see and be seen, Jesus was there to observe what others deemed as insignificant. The other observers looked for abundance, Jesus looked for attitude. The subject of observation for most was what was in the **hand** of men, but Jesus looked for what was in the **heart** of men. This truth can be seen when God sent Samuel to anoint the next King of Israel to replace Saul who He had rejected. Instructed to go to the house of Jessie, Samuel began to examine the sons of Jessie and was sure he had found a suitable successor in Jessie's oldest son *(I Samuel 16:6)*. Samuel went looking for height and God was looking for heart! *"But the LORD said unto Samuel, Look not on his countenance, or on the height of his stature; because I have refused him: for the LORD* *seeth not as man seeth; for man looketh on the outward appearance, but the LORD looketh on the heart" (I Samuel 16:7).* The Bible tells us that God *"trieth the hearts" (Proverbs 17:3), "knoweth the hearts" (Acts 15:8), "searcheth the hearts" (Romans 8:27)*, and will one day *"make manifest the counsels of the hearts" (I Corinthians 4:5).* When others were looking at the actions of man's hand, Jesus was observing the attitude of man's heart!

Mark said that Jesus *"sat over against the treasury, and beheld" (Mark 12:41).* The word *"beheld"* means that Jesus became a spectator, to discern or consider. What was it that Jesus was observing or trying to see? We find the **standard of observation** in the text then it says, *"beheld how."* The definition of *"how"* is in what way or manner, how much, or by what means. The standard that man uses for equating the value of an offering is drastically different from the standard that God uses. The natural eye could only see the **substance** of the offering. The disciples, as well as other onlookers, could only assign a dollar amount to the individual gifts as they were dropped into the coffers. These observers could only view things from the outward perspective. The higher the dollar amount the greater the offering and the greater the praise heaped upon the individual. The people looked to see how much was given but Jesus looked to see how much was left. He looked at the **sacrifice** of the offering. What did it cost that individual to give what they gave? There was a young man in my first church that was the preacher's buddy. He was around seven years old and he had captured my heart. He would go with me on Tuesdays to visit shut-ins and just enjoyed hanging around with his preacher. One day before Sunday school his mother told me that the young man had something for me. He reached into his pocket and pulled out a $5.00 bill. This was money that he had saved for himself. He had asked his mother if he could give his preacher one of his Abraham Lincoln's, a $5.00 bill. She told me that she approved and wanted me to have it. Humbly I took the bill and put it in a small treasure chest at home. It would be a life long treasure from a very special person. Some time later a preacher came to our area in an evangelist campaign. God placed His hand upon the meeting and it continued for several weeks and had even expanded to morning services. In one of the night services a special need arose and I felt impressed to give everything in my wallet. Feeling confident that I had done all I could do I focused on the service. Then a still small voice spoke to my heart and said, "you still have something to give." I thought to myself, I don't have a single cent, I have given everything! Then I remember the $5.00 in the chest at home and the still small voice said, "That's what I want." The next morning I placed it in the hands of the preacher conducting the services. While he only saw the substance, God saw the sacrifice. A true blessing only comes when one learns to give in accordance to God's standard and not that of man!

In Luke's account of the widow's offering, he makes an interesting statement about our Lord's observation of what was taking place, *"And he looked up, and saw the rich men casting their gift . . . And he saw also a certain widow" (Luke 21:1-2).* The word *"saw"* tells us something of the **scrutiny of observation**. The word means to see or know, to be aware, to perceive and have full knowledge or understanding. Some observers may have come to the wrong conclusion about the offerings being placed into the individual trumpets, but not our Lord. There was nothing that would get by the scrutinizing eye of the Son of God. He had full knowledge of **each person**. Being God, He knew where that person lived, their age, their height, their weight, and their status in life. He even had the hairs of their head numbered. That knowledge is not just limited to a few, but includes every one of Adam's race. Jesus knew **each present** that was dropped into the trumpets. While the two mites were so small that most had no idea what the poor widow deposited, Jesus knew! Jesus was totally aware of every gift of every person. He even has a record of cups of water given in His name *(Mark 9:41)*. As the people parade by depositing things into the trumpets, Jesus is aware of **each purpose** behind the gift. He has full knowledge between showmanship, and sacrifice. While it may not be distinguishable to others He knows if the gift is that of love or loftiness.

May each of us be mindful of the fact that others are observing our lives. What they see in us shapes many of their values and beliefs. But, we must never forget that of all those that observe us, the Lord is the most knowledgeable and discerning judge. He is watching and keeping a record that we will one day face. Nothing can be hid from His all Seeing Eye!

(III) The Overview – *"this poor widow hath cast more in, than all"*

While the offerer may have been silent, the observer was not! The widow's faith must be acknowledged. What she had done in secret, would be rewarded openly *(see Matthew 6:4)*. Her act of faith would be rewarded by a **visible exaltation**, *"And he called unto him his disciples" (Mark 12:43)*. This poor widow had tried to remain hidden within the crowd. Edersheim said of the approach, "alone as if ashamed to mingle with the crowd of rich givers, ashamed to have her offering seen, perhaps ashamed to bring it; a 'widow', in the garb of a desolate mourner, her condition, appearance, bearing that of a 'pauper.'" While she would not draw attention to herself, Jesus would not allow her to pass by unnoticed. Jesus called for the attention of His disciples and singled the little widow out. She may have not caught the eye of the Rabbis or the rich, but she would be noticed because Jesus would see to it. There is a day coming when a lot of unknowns shall be made known! At the judgment seat of Christ, before an innumerable host, each one of God's children will pass before Him. In that day the secrets of the heart as well as the secret habits of each one will be made manifest. Many that have failed to gain the applause or the attention of religion will be exposed for their great faith. Some that have been used to the limelight will be dwarfed and pushed into the shadows as the unknowns are being made known.

The widow received a **vocal exaltation** from the Lord Jesus, *"Verily I say unto you, That this poor widow hath cast more in, than all they which have cast into the treasury" (Mark 12:43)*. The rich's *"much" (vs.42)* was overshadowed by the widow's *"more" (vs.43)*. The poor widow had put in two mites. A mite was the smallest of the copper coins, one eighth of a cent. Her offering was equal to the farthing, a Roman coin valued at one forth of a cent. Her offering was the very least offering allowed by the Rabbinical rules. When contrasting the offerings, Jesus said, *"cast more in, than all."* She had given more in quantity as well as quality. How could this be? How could least by man's standard be the most by God's standard? When others looked at the **gift** God looked at the **giver**. The rich cast in of their abundance or the super abounding overflow *(see Luke 21:4)*. A gift they never missed. This was not the case with the woman's gift. Luke describes her as a *"poor widow" (Luke 21:2)* and said of her, *"but she of her penury hath cast in all the living that she had" (Luke 21:4)*. Putting all this together Luke is saying that this person of desperate need that lacked a husband to provide for her in a state of deficit, a present state of existence by implying the means of livelihood gave until there was nothing left to give. It was this type of giving faith that brought forth praise from the lips of the Saviour. Will we hear Him say, *"Well done, thou good and faithful servant: thou hast been faithful over a few things, I will make thee ruler over many things: enter thou into the joy of thy lord" (Matthew 25:21)*?

This was a **valuable exaltation**, *"And he called . . . and saith" (Mark 12:43)*. This was not the exaltation of mere mortals; this was her master that sang her praises! The value of the praise is determined by the quality of the character of the one giving praise. In *Matthew 6*, Jesus tells of a group of individuals that *"love to pray standing in the synagogues and in the corners of the streets, that they may be seen of men" (vs.5)*. These individuals made themselves vocal and visible so that they might receive the exaltations of men. Jesus said, concerning this act of hypocrisy, *"Verily I say unto you, They have their reward."* This poor widow valued the exaltation of God above that of mortal men. Whom do you desire the praises of, men or the Master?

This poor little widow slipped through the crowd and dropped in an offering that caught the eye of the Eternal and that was recorded for eternity. The fruit of her hands was nothing more than the manifestation of the faith within her heart! Faith is concerned with action rather than applause. While it was the smallest in size, it was the greatest in significance. It was not the size of the gift that caught the eye of Jesus, but rather the sacrifice of the giver. While true faith may not always be vocal to the ear it is vibrant and visible to the discerning eye. One may display works without faith, but one cannot have faith that does not work. Though her faith was silent to the ear it spoke volumes to the eye, especially those of her Saviour.

Chapter Nine

The Sufficiency of Faith

Matthew 15:28 "Then Jesus answered and said unto her, O woman, great is thy faith: be it unto thee even as thou wilt. And her daughter was made whole from that very hour."

Confronted with the verbal retribution of the scribes and Pharisees over the traditions of men, Jesus responds with truth that reveals the shallowness of their love and the sinfulness of their devotion. Because of the spiritual immaturity of His disciples our Lord must enlighten them to the depravity of the human heart. After encouraging those present to turn from damnable traditions unto divine truth Jesus departs to the borders of Tyre and Sidon. Jesus had made His way there in an effort to be hid and obtain some much-needed rest *(see Mark 7:24)*. But, there was an even greater reason behind this journey! It was a journey of divine appointment. It was much like his journey to meet the Samaritan women at the well of Sychar. *"He left Judaea, and departed again into Galilee. And he must needs go through Samaria" (John 4:3-4).* In the journey to Samaria, the will of the Heavenly Father is revealed in the phrase, *"He must needs."* It was the divine plan of God for Jesus to confront a Samaritan woman with a **sinful character**, and it was also the Sovereign's will to comfort a Syrophenician woman with a **sick child**. Both women would find in Christ a sufficient and satisfactory answer to their need! Herbert Lockyer said, "He goes to the borders of Tyre and Sidon for a single deed of mercy toward one outside of the Holy Land."

Arriving at the coasts of Tyre and Sidon, Jesus is met by a woman crying for **mercy** and looking for a **miracle**. *"Have mercy on me, O Lord, thou son of David; my daughter is grievously vexed with a devil" (Matthew 15:22).* Armed with faith this woman of Canaan came to the only one that could supply her with what she needed. What a delight to her ears to hear the Master say, *"O woman, great is thy faith: be it unto thee even as thou wilt."* She, like so many others, would discover the **sufficiency of faith.** In her plight, this brokenhearted mother would make two great discoveries: faith was all she had and faith was all she needed.

(I) Faith's Conquest

Whether it is in the Garden of Eden or the daily grind of everyday life, faith will never go unchallenged. James referred to this conflict as *"the trying of your faith"* while Peter called it *"the trial of your faith" (James 1:3, I Peter 1:7).* Faith will not be permitted to magnify the Saviour and exalt His Word without a full-scale war with the opposing forces! The faith of our first parents were challenged by the **words of Satan** with a subtle suggestion, *"Yea, hath God said" (Genesis 3:1).* Could God be trusted to have our best interests at heart? The faith of the disciples was met by the **winds of the storm**. They had been commanded, *"get into the ship, and to go to the other side before unto Bethsaida" (Mark 6:45),* while He sent the multitude away. Could God be trusted to be their guide? The saint is challenged in their faith by the **wisdom of the senses** when they heard, *"Give, and it shall be given unto you; good measure, pressed down, and shaken together, and running over, shall men give into your bosom" (Luke 6:38).* Can one trust God for daily provisions if one becomes a channel for blessings rather than a reservoir? The **willfulness of the sinner** opposes faith in the Lord Jesus Christ for a full salvation. Can man get to heaven on the unmerited favor and mercy of God, which was manifested, in the finished work of His Son on Calvary?

The natural instinct of the human heart is to cry in unison with the voices of those in the wilderness, *"Can God?" (Psalm 78:19).* Faith will be challenged and the faith of this mother will be no different! If this woman's faith was to flourish, it must show itself superior in the conquest of **travel**. Jesus made His way down to the borders of Tyre and Sidon. Matthew tells us *"a woman of Canaan came out of the same coasts" (15:22)*. Jesus came down to the corner where blind Bartimaeus was setting *(Mark 10:46)*. Jesus stopped underneath the tree that Zacchceus had climbed and commanded him to come down *(Luke 19:5)*. Jesus was waiting on the woman of Sychar when she arrived at the well *(John 4:7)*. But the Syrophenician woman would have to go to where Jesus was! She would have to conquer the length of the journey. We do not know the exact distance that she had to travel, but the fact remains that she was willing to go any distance to get to Jesus. She must conquer the loneliness of the journey. From Mark's account, it appears that she left her daughter behind and made her way to Jesus. She had not brought the burden in hand, but she had bore it in her heart. With nothing but the anguish of her daughter's condition weighing heavily upon her, in solitude she made her way to Jesus.

She would face the conquest of **tradition**. Tradition erected two barriers that must be conquered. One was her gender and the other was the fact that she was a Gentile. Men usually did not converse with women in public places and this was especially true if the man occupied a sacred position. As a Gentile she occupied a position outside the commonwealth of Israel, the chosen people of God. Herbert Lockyer said, "By calling her a woman of Canaan it meant that she was a descendant of the original inhabitants of Canaan, she was a Gentile of the Gentiles. The nation she represented was marked by divine judgments, and its guilt had risen up to God and cried out for vengeance, and retribution fell upon it." After breaking His silence, Jesus informed her *"I am not sent but unto the lost sheep of the house of Israel" (Matthew 15:24)*. Yet, she would not be denied access to the only one that could help her. Charging against tradition this gentile woman broke through the barriers to receive a blessing.

There would be the conquest of **training.** If faith was to reign supreme, it must conquer the training of her past. Being a

Phoenician, she would have worshipped the great mother-goddess, "Ashtoreth" or "Astarte" or "Queen of heaven," giver of all life in plant, animal and man. This goddess was supposed to give everything good to her devoted followers. The devotees were permitted to indulge in almost everything evil. This idolatrous gentile woman must turn from a god unto the True and Living God. By coming to Christ she would be denouncing the false gods of her past and she would be believing *"that he is, and that he is a rewarder of them that diligently seek him" (Hebrews 11:6).*

The faith of this grief-stricken mother would prove to be superior to all that would challenge it. Just as she was met with the conquest of faith, so will each of us! Peter warned of this daily challenge when he wrote, *"Beloved, think it not strange concerning the fiery trial which is to try you, as though some strange thing happened unto you" (I Peter 4:12).*

(II) Faith's Counterfeit

Our hearts are caused to rejoice as faith triumphs turning the search for mercy and a miracle into salutations of peace and praise. As we follow the plight of this burdened mother we watch as this gentile's faith was proven to be true Biblical faith and not a counterfeit. If you are not careful you can possibly mistake **ripe fruit** for the **real faith**. Many have become so preoccupied with faith's fragrant blossoms that they forget the root from which it flourishes! This preoccupation has caused a lot of individuals to make a counterfeit for faith and then wonder why it will not spend in the bank of heaven.

Some are guilty of making **words** a counterfeit for real faith. Have you ever said, or heard someone else say, "I don't understand. I said all the right words and even prayed in Jesus' name and nothing happened." The fact that you are questioning yourself tells you where your confidence was when you sought help. I said, I prayed, faith does not look to you for the answer. Faith looks to Him!

While she may have been a Gentile, a stranger to the covenant of God, and was raised in a nation that knew not the True and Living God, she knew all the right words to say. She knew what to ask for, *"Have mercy on me (Matthew 15:22).* It was not the words of a stern requirement, but rather a sympathetic request! She is not making demands of Him, but rather placing the burden of her heart at Jesus' feet. She was aware of the various titles by which Jesus was called. He was the Lord; He was supreme in authority and controller of all things. He was the son of David, the Messiah, the promised seed, the true King of Israel. This Syrophenician woman used all the correct terms. She was in need of mercy and He was everything she had said He was. Yet, it was not her words that **solidified** her faith, it was her faith that **seasoned** her words. This would have been a valuable lesson for the rich young ruler to have learned before he approached the Lord. It was not the young man's words, but his wickedness that kept him from receiving salvation.

It is possible to make **works** a counterfeit for faith. Have you ever thought or heard it said, "I read my Bible, go to church, tithe, and do the best I can. Why isn't it working?" If there was one thing that could be said about this woman, it is she did all the right things! Works marks the whole account of this woman and her daughter's healing. She leaves the country of her birth in a wearisome journey of countless days to find Christ. For several days she follows our Lord's disciples until they want Him to just give her what she wants to get rid of her. She makes her way into the house He is residing and confronts the Master again. There are religious works revealed in denouncing her national gods and the act of worship as she falls before Him. Surely she has labored enough to merit a blessing! Remember it is mercy and not merit! It is not works that **guarantees** faith; rather it is faith that **generates** works.

I am not minimizing the importance of our words and our works so long as you do not make them a substitute for true Biblical faith. The fragrant flowers of words and the fruit of works are the product of the plant of faith that is nourished by the Word of God. Do not accept a counterfeit for the real thing.

(III) Faith's Character

Webster's dictionary defines character as a distinctive trait or quality, one's pattern of behavior. While others may act like faith, faith will only act one way! Faith will display its distinctive traits and behave accordingly. The faith of the Syrophenician woman displayed the faultless character of true Biblical faith. There are two elements of faith's character that I want to magnify from this account.

In this story we see the **persistence of faith**. Faith has eradicated the word quit from its vocabulary. Faith does not end a sentence with a question mark! Faith does not think so, faith knows so! Because of this, faith will persevere in spite of things seen and unseen. When it comes to all the obstacles that this mother faced as she sought for mercy and a miracle most would have given up. Most would have returned home satisfied and comforted with the thought of, I tried and what more could have been done? Like Jacob she said within her soul, *"I will not let thee go, except thou bless me" (Genesis 32:26).* When one thinks of faith's perseverance we need to be mindful of the words of Richard Trench, "when we speak on man overcoming God, we must never for an instant lose sight of this, that the power whereby he overcomes the resistance of God, is itself a power supplied by God." In the New Testament we are admonished by the Lord Himself, *"Ask, and it shall be given you; seek, and ye shall find; knock, and it shall be opened unto you" (Luke 11:9).* I am told that the thought here is, ask and keep on asking, knock and keep on knocking. There is the admonishment to persevere! In *Luke 18* our Lord tells the parable of the unjust judge and the widow. She was avenged because of her persistence. True Faith will not quit.

This burdened soul would not quit when confronted with the **scorn of men**, *"Send her away; for she crieth after us" (Matthew 15:23).* The disciples had gotten tired of this continual obnoxious cry. She had become an embarrassment to them. Here is a woman continually interrupting their rest. They knew people were asking questions and saying things. Secondly, she is not one of us. She is a gentile that comes from heathen background that should have perished under the condemnation of a Holy God and we cannot get rid of her. She saw their looks of contempt! She heard the malicious and cruel things they said about her! But, she had a daughter that had more than a common cold. The child of her womb was grievously vexed by an evil spirit and faith would not let go.

She was persistent in spite of the **silence of the Master**, *"But he answered her not a word" (Matthew 15:23).* The words of men are difficult enough to take, but some times the silence is worst. One writer said, " 'The Word' had no word for her aching heart." While others would be discouraged, faith was encouraged. While there had been no positive word of encouragement, there had been no negative word of discouragement! This was the battle that was fought in the souls of Mary and Martha as they waited upon Jesus to come and heal their sick brother, Lazarus *(see John 11).* There had been four days of silence waiting for the Master to come and assert His authority over this sickness. Faith will not only embrace the Master's ways, but the Master's waiting.

She would not succumb to defeat despite the **size of the miracle**, *"my daughter is grievously vexed with a devil" (Matthew 15:22).* G. Campbell Morgan said, "The language implies that she was badly demonized." How would we answer the question given to aged Abraham and barren Sarah when they were told they would have the son of promise, *"Is any thing too hard for the LORD" (Genesis 18:14)?* Is there anything that lies outside the boundaries of God's power? Burdened for her dear distressed daughter this mother does not allow the magnitude of the need to stop her but rather it strengthens her persevering spirit. She would not be deterred! The Lord told his disciples that mountains could be removed, trees uprooted and planted in the sea by the simple faith as a grain of mustard seed *(see Matthew 17:20, Luke 17:6)*. By placing limits on our faith we are placing limits on our God. May we say in unison with Jeremiah, *"Ah Lord GOD! behold, thou hast made the heaven and the earth by thy great power and stretched out arm, and there is nothing too hard for thee" (Jeremiah 32:17).*

Spurgeon said, "He tried her faith by His silence and by His discouraging replies, that he might see its strength; but he was all the while delighting in it, and secretly sustaining it, and when He had sufficiently tried it, He brought it forth as gold, and set His own royal mark upon it in these memorable words, *'O woman, great is thy faith, be it unto thee even as thou wilt.'* "

The character of faith is marked by the **perception of faith**. Faith is not some blind leap into the darkness. Because faith is established on the truth of God's Word there is illumination. The Psalmist said, *"Thy word is a lamp unto my feet, and a light unto my path" (Psalm 119:105).* We also read in *Proverbs 6:23, "For the commandment is a lamp; and the law is light."* There are four references in the New Testament to the *"children of light."* Because we are children of the light, we have illumination, which increases the opportunity for perception. The precious mother was permitted to see **self**. Much like the Centurion with the sick servant who constantly cried unworthy, this woman saw the lowliness of self. When the master contrasted the rights of children to that of the dogs, she immediately took the lower position, *"It is not meet to take the children's bread, and cast it to dogs" (Matthew 15:26).* But the light revealed an even greater truth about her depravity and she readily confessed it. There is a difference in the word Jesus used for dog and the word the woman used for dog. Jesus was saying that it was not right to take the allotted food of the children and feed it to the household pet, the little puppy that roamed about the house. The woman of Canaan made reference to the wild scavenger dogs that ran lose in the streets and hillsides of the country. These dogs were malnourished, infested with parasites and eaten up with disease. Considered a menace to society these dogs were deemed worthless. She would approach the Lord Jesus Christ on the merit of His mercy!

There was illumination on the **Saviour**. The object of the woman's faith would be Jesus! This cannot be overstated! Greater perception into the person of Jesus only magnifies the opportunities for greater faith. In approaching Jesus, this woman uses two titles to describe Him. When she calls Him the *"son of David"* she magnifies Him as **prophet** and **potentate**. One writer pointed out that in using this title she knew Him to be the Prophet of Nazareth. He was the inspired speaker of divine truth. She sought Him out because of His Word. The title also implies that Jesus was Israel's Messiah, the king that would liberate His people and occupy the throne. There was the perception of His right to rule. When she referred to Him as *"Lord"* there was the perception of His **power**. He was the one of supreme authority over all things. Should not such a one rightfully be the single object of her faith?

Faith also had a perception of the **sickness**. Her daughter's sickness became her sickness! G. Campbell Morgan said, "Here she is making her child's misery her own. There was only one soul and one interest between them, they were bound together." Many times the weakness of our faith is because we do not identify with the need or burden of another. This kind of attitude makes our prayer nothing more than a frivolous request rather than a passionate desire. Paul said in *Galatians 6:2 "Bear ye one another's burdens, and so fulfil the law of Christ."* The intensity of her request and the strength of the union between her and the daughter's need can be seen in her words to Christ, *"Have mercy on me, O Lord" (Matthew 15:22)*. The heart-felt pleas of this mother reveal her affection for her very dear, distressed daughter. She did not say, "Have mercy on us" or "Have mercy on her." She must have a miracle from God!

Her lowliness only served to magnify His loftiness. The perception of the sickness caused her to not only identify with the need, but also generated a persistence that would not stop until she got her burden to the Lord. What was it that caused her to behave in such a manner? It was faith, for true Biblical faith will manifest its true character.

Facing the conquest and not accepting any counterfeits, this woman's faith persevered on to victory in Christ. She had discovered that faith was not only all she had, but it was all she needed. One old preacher said, "True prayers never come weeping home." There is the **sufficiency** of true Biblical faith.

Chapter Ten

The Success of Faith

Luke 5:20 "And when he saw their faith, he said unto him, Man, thy sins are forgiven thee."

When speaking of the virtues of charity, Paul said, *"Beareth all things, believeth all things, hopeth all things, endureth all things. Charity never faileth" (1 Corinthians 13:7-8).* What can be said of charity can also be said of faith. True Biblical faith will never fail; it will succeed! Faith will not leave one sinner marooned on the isle of condemnation. *"For whosoever shall call upon the name of the Lord shall be saved" (Romans 10:13). "Come unto me, all ye that labour and are heavy laden, and I will give you rest" (Matthew 11:28).* Faith will not leave one saint abandoned in the valley of conflict. *Call unto me, and I will answer thee, and show thee great and mighty things, which thou knowest not" (Jeremiah 33:3).* David said, *"I have been young, and now am old; yet have I not seen the righteous forsaken, nor his seed begging bread. He is ever merciful, and lendeth; and his seed is blessed" (Psalm 37:25-26).* Faith will save the sinner and sustain the saint! One never goes wrong when they approach God in faith.

In *Luke 5:17-26,* the success of faith is magnified to its fullest potential. The corporate act of faith in the lives of five men succeed in tapping into the bountiful blessings of God. One sick of the palsy and four other men approach Christ by faith. Four carry the man and his bed in while the man that was sick of the palsy carries his bed out. Faith had been successful in **saving** the thief on the cross, **strengthening** David in the valley of Elah, **supplying** Peter with fish from the sea, and **silencing** the false prophets on Mount Carmel. Faith had not failed others and it would not fail these five men that put their faith in the Lord

Jesus Christ. Faith will succeed and will not fail because the object of faith, the Lord God Jehovah, cannot fail.

(I) The Marks of Success - *vs.19&20*

While there are numerous things that mark a faith that is successful and will succeed, I want to center our attention on two dominant marks within the text. One mark that magnifies a faith that will succeed is **the persistence of the seeker**. When one reads the entire account of the man sick with the palsy, it is evident that these five men are met at every turn by opposition. If the sick of the palsy is to be healed, he must get to the object of faith. *"They sought means to bring him in, and to lay him before him" (Luke 5:18).* If faith was to succeed it must overcome the **magnitude of the need**. This man could not get to Jesus by himself for his defective limbs would not transport him into the Lord's presence. He was unlike one with a withered hand, deaf ear, or a silent tongue that could make their way to Jesus. The man sick of the palsy could have echoed the words of the man by the pool of Bethesda, *"Sir, I have no man" (John 5:7).* Thanks be unto God, there was a man that shared his faith and saw his need. The sick of the palsy would need more than one individual to aid him. Unlike one that was blind, which could be led by a single individual, this man would require at least four to carry him upon his bed. This reminds us of God's precious promise, *"That if two of you shall agree on earth as touching any thing that they shall ask, it shall be done for them of my Father which is in heaven" (Matthew 18:19).* What a blessing to have others that are sensitive to your needs and willing to help shoulder the load. When I think of the unity that should be among the family of God, there are two verses that come to my mind. *"Brethren, if a man be overtaken in a fault, ye which are spiritual, restore such an one in the spirit of meekness; considering thyself, lest thou also be tempted. Bear ye one another's burdens, and so fulfil the law of Christ" (Galatians 6:1-2).* Motivated by the Word and a warning, each of us should actively look for opportunities to minister to others.

Cooperating as a unit, these men of like faith make their way to Jesus, only to be opposed by **men in the way**, *"many were gathered together, insomuch that there was no room to receive them, no, not so much as about the door" (Mark 2:2).* From what we can gather from the two accounts *(Mark 2:1-12, Luke 5:17-26),* there are far more people obstructing the way to Jesus than opening the way to Jesus. There is a very large number that have come from great distances *(see Luke 5:17&21)* to scrutinize the words, works, and ways of our Lord. They are not there to receive a blessing, but rather to buffet His conduct and character. These self-righteous whited sepulchers have no need for Him and will not direct one needy soul unto Him. In many cases, our apathy impedes others from getting to Christ. Each of us is either part of the way or we are in the way!

Not to be stopped these men of faith move to the roof and find **materials that need to be removed**, *"they uncovered the roof where he was: and when they had broken it up, they let down the bed" (Mark 2:4).* Some times the material things of this world hinder our faith. This is what happened to the young ruler that came to Jesus, *"Good Master, what shall I do that I may inherit eternal life?" (Mark 10:17).* Jesus told him to go and sell all that he had, give it to the poor and come and follow Him. What was the young man's response, *"And he was sad at that saying, and went away grieved: for he had great possessions" (Mark 10:22).* He was not willing to remove the materials of this world that faith might succeed. This is also truth in the life of one of God's children, a man named Demas. Paul said, *"Demas hath forsaken me, having loved this present world, and is departed unto Thessalonica" (II Timothy 4:10).* Are there any materials that you are not willing to breakup and cast aside that your faith might succeed?

The success of faith is marked by **the perception of the Sovereign**, *"And when he saw their faith" (Luke 5:20).* There are numerous times that others are permitted to see our faith. When Peter and John were brought before Annas the high priest, those in attendance saw the faith of these two disciples. *"Now when they saw the boldness of Peter and John, and perceived that they were unlearned and ignorant men, they marvelled; and they took knowledge of them, that they had been with Jesus" (Acts 4:13).* The strength of our witness before a lost and dying world is in their ability to see our faith. If that which is projected as faith is true faith, it must be seen by more than just society. If it is true faith, the Sovereign as well as society will see it. There are great numbers of folks that project the appearance of faith. Society sees it and accepts it as faith but God does not see it as true faith. Their acts are nothing more than elaborate showmanship. While there are times that our faith is seen by the Sovereign and not by society, there is never a time that true faith is seen by society and not the Sovereign.

Mesmerized by their substance and showmanship, the disciples kept a constant eye upon those of means. While the others had their eye upon the wealthy, Jesus was drawn to a widow *(see Mark 12:41-44)*. If it had not been for the Lord Jesus Christ, she would have slipped in and out undetected by his disciples and her act of sacrifice would have been unknown. Others were moved by fortunes and Jesus was touched by faith. It was of greater importance to catch the discerning eye of the Sovereign than the deceitful eye of society.

In response to the cry for help, Jesus proceeds to the house of Jairus. A great multitude followed Him to see a great feat, but one followed to exhibit great faith *(see Mark 5:24-34)*. Others are thronging Him, but she desires only to touch Him. Slowly she weaves and maneuvers her way to within arm's reach. There within that great host of folks faith touches the border of His garment and immediately the issue of blood is dried up. Her act of faith had remained undetected by the multitude, but it had not escaped the discernment of the Master, *"Who touched my clothes?" (Mark 5:30).* His disciples responded by saying, *"Thou seest the multitude thronging thee, and sayest thou, Who touched me?" (Mark 5:31).* The disciples saw the touch of all men the same, but not our Lord. He had been touched by more than a hand; He had been touched with the heart!

In *Matthew 6*, Jesus tells His disciples about a faulty faith that is exhibited in the giving of alms and the act of prayer. There are those that give *"that they may have glory of men" (vs.2)*, those that pray so *"that they may be seen of men" (vs.5)*. Jesus said of that kind of faith, *"They have their reward" (vs. 2&5)*. These individuals were motivated by the attention and applause of men. Exposure was their reason for doing it and that was what they were rewarded with. The flesh rewards seductive faith and the Father rewards secretive faith *(see vs. 6)*.

It is far better to have our Lord acknowledge the evidence of faith than expose the error of faith. True faith may go unnoticed by society and even the saints; but it will never escape the discerning eye of the Sovereign. The widow's mite and the woman's touch were rewarded, while the rich man's extravagance is ridiculed. The persistent seeker that gains the perception of the Sovereign will always see their faith succeed.

(II) The Materializing of Success - *vs.20&25*
True faith will accomplish its task and be rewarded! Listen closely to this phrase, *"when he saw their faith, he said" (Luke 5:20)*. Just as soon as those men had gotten to Jesus and their faith was revealed, their faith was rewarded, *"he saw . . . he said."* The operation of faith was answered by the omnipotence of God. This great truth is made evident throughout the Word of God. The woman of Canaan that had a daughter that was vexed with a devil came to Jesus in faith. As soon as her faith was seen, *"O woman, great is thy faith" (Matthew 15:28)*, the Bible said, *"And her daughter was made whole from that very hour."* When faith was manifested, success materialized!

In *John 4*, a nobleman comes to Jesus in behalf of his son who is dying. Jesus confronted the man about true faith, *"Except ye see signs and wonders, ye will not believe" (John 4:48)*. The man responds with a compassionate cry for the life of his son. Jesus turns to the man and said, *"Go thy way; thy son liveth" (vs.50)*. By faith the father believes the words of the Lord Jesus and went his way. The next day the nobleman is met by one of his servants with the good news of his son's recovery. The man inquires as to the time of the boy's recovery. The servant replied, *"Yesterday at the seventh hour the fever left him" (vs.52)*. The Bible said, *"So the father knew that it was at the same hour, in the which Jesus said unto him, Thy son liveth: and himself believed, and his whole house" (vs.53)*. When the man surrendered to the Word in faith, success materialized.

This same great truth can be seen in the matter of salvation. *"For God so loved the world, that he gave his only begotten Son, that whosoever believeth in him should not perish, but have everlasting life" (John 3:16). "For whosoever shall call upon the name of the Lord shall be saved" (Romans 10:13)*. When a sinner responds in faith to the message of the gospel of Jesus Christ, they have eternal life. That individual that was dead has been quickened and made alive in the Lord Jesus Christ. Paul tells us that God *"hath quickened us together with Christ, (by grace ye are saved;) And hath raised us up together, and made us sit together in heavenly places in Christ Jesus" (Ephesians 2:5-6)*. Faith's success materializes in **security**, *"And I give unto them eternal life; and they shall never perish, neither shall any man pluck them out of my hand. My Father, which gave them me, is greater than all; and no man is able to pluck them out of my Father's hand" (John 10:28-29)*. Even though the believer is still in this physical tabernacle, he is positionally seated in heavenly places in Christ. He is just waiting for the adoption, the redemption of the body *(see Romans 8:23)*. The believer is just waiting to possess what has already been accomplished by the operation of faith. Faith's success materializes in **surety**. The work of Christ will be brought to completion in the life of the child of God. *"Being confident of this very thing, that he which hath begun a good work in you will perform it until the day of Jesus Christ" (Philippians 1:6)*. The noble man and the woman of Canaan had to reach home to see with the natural eye what faith accomplished. The success of faith had materialized in the healing of a son and of a daughter the day the parents responded in faith to the words of Jesus, even if the parents had to wait to see it.

The greatest exhibition of the materialization of faith's success is most likely *Hebrews 11*. In this one chapter the phrase *"by faith"* is used sixteen times in fifteen verses. Faith was successful in producing a quality **witness** in the life of Abel *(see vs.4)*. It was Abel's faith that caused him to offer the sacrifice of a lamb, rather than a sacrifice of the land.

Faith's success materialized a **walk** for Enoch *(vs.5)*, a **warning** for Noah *(vs.7)*, a **willingness** for Abraham *(vs.8&9)*, **worship** for Jacob *(vs.21)*, **warfare** for believers *(vs.23-30)*, and a **worthiness** for the persecuted *(vs. 38)*.

Faith's success not only materialized in the lives those best known as the heroes of the Old Testament, but it materialized among the common and unknown individuals of faith. For many there is no name attached to their acts of faith, but that makes no difference in the outcome, *"And these all, having obtained a good report through faith" (vs.39)*. For all that will respond in faith to the promises of God, faith will succeed. The operation of faith cannot fail because the object of our faith cannot fail.

(III) The Message of Success – vs.25-26
The tiling of the roof is broken up and the bed upon which the man with the palsy is let down into the presence of our Lord. After silencing and shaming the scribes and Pharisees *(see vs.21-24)*, Jesus turns and speaks to the man sick of the palsy, *"I say unto thee, Arise, and take up thy couch, and go into thine house" (vs.24)*. The man responds immediately to the command of Jesus as strength surges through his limbs. He picks up his bed and departs for his own house. Faith's success has been manifested to not just the five men that were operating in faith, but unto all

those assembled about the Lord Jesus Christ. When the success of faith was manifested, it projected a message.

There was a **vocal message**, *"departed . . . glorifying God. And they . . . glorified God . . . saying, We have seen."* After seeing what faith had accomplished, all those with an honest heart gave a vocal message. I have heard the text, *Luke 5:17-26*, preached on several times. Without exception, the main subject of every message was the four men that brought the man sick of the palsy to Jesus. The messages have been directed at responsibility, concern, and unity. All these things are good and necessary, but this was not the message of successful faith. When the message went forth it was not the four men that everyone spoke of, but rather, it was a message about Him. Faith does not magnify man it magnifies the Master.

The message magnifies His person, *"glorifying God."* Rising to his feet, he that had been sick of the palsy, began to render and esteem God glorious and worthy of all honors. As he exited the room, the crowd joins him in unison. They were giving praise to the one that had wrought such a great miracle and that person was Jesus. What was the subject of this praise? I believe they were esteeming Him as being God *(Theos)*, a deity, the Supreme Divinity. They were persuaded in their hearts that only God could do such things. If that were the case, then Jesus must be God. When faith succeeded in one's life or is seen in the life of another, we will not elevate the individual, but rather, praise the True and Living God that doeth all things well. If faith is to succeed its object must be God and when faith's success materializes, God will be the object of praise.

The message magnifies His power, *"strange things."* When the people saw all that had transpired, they said, *"We have seen strange things to day."* What did that group of people mean when they spoke of seeing *"strange things"*? The phrase means in the sense of seeming contrary to expectation, extraordinary. I do not know that it was what they expected, but the actions and

126

the abilities of Jesus surprised them. What Jesus was able to do was contrary to the **norm** and to **nature**. What the people had just witnessed superseded what they expected from a rabbi or a religious service. Jesus was breaking all the stereotypes of traditional religious ways. It was also extraordinary that He could control nature and have it do His bidding. Sickness was replaced with strength and the cripple was made capable.

Unified as one voice the man and the multitude praise Jesus for His power and His person. He is God and they praise Him as such. When God responds to our faith in Him and success materializes before us, what are the subject and the substance of our message?

There was a **visible message**, *"he rose up before them . . . and departed to his own . . . they were all amazed . . . and were filled with fear."* The multitude not only responded with a message, but they were the recipients of a message. When Jesus saw their faith, He spoke, and when He spoke there was substance. Everyone immediately saw faith's success materialize before him or her. They were not just hearing a message, *"Arise, and take up thy couch"*, they saw a message, *"And immediately he rose up before them."* They received not only a message through the ear gate, but also the eye gate.

There was the visible message of **an act, an amazement**, and **an alarm**. When they saw the man rise to his feet, pick up his bed, and depart, this act was a message from God to their intellect. To the mind of man, everything that they were seeing with their eyes was contrary to the natural man. Like Nicodemus they would be quick to say, *"How can these things be?" (John 3:9)*. This was an act contrary to the ways and works of man.

The visible message spoke to their emotions for Luke said; *"they were all amazed."* The word *"amazed"* means a displacement of the mind, bewilderment, astonished, trance. They are so touched by the fact that God has been made manifest by such a mighty work they are mesmerized. They cannot describe what they are feeling. The message has spoken to their spirit for fear has risen up in their hearts and they are alarmed. They have come face to face with God. Like Gideon, they could say, *"Alas, O Lord GOD! for because I have seen an angel of the LORD face to face" (Judges 6:22)*. They had found themselves in the presence of the Supreme Divinity.

God had delivered a visible message that spoke to their intellect, emotions, and spirit. By doing this, God had equipped each of them with all they needed to respond to Him in saving faith and sustaining faith.

Armed with nothing but faith, these five men persevered and got their burden to Jesus. When *"Jesus saw . . . he said"* and faith's success materialized. True faith will not fail! Faith had not failed all those that had come before them and it would not fail them. The materializing of faith's success generated a vocal message that magnifies the Sovereign and not the sinner. It generated a visible message from God that equips all to appropriate true faith. True Bible faith will succeed in saving the sinner and sustaining the saint.